Pictures of Cocks, ENJOY!

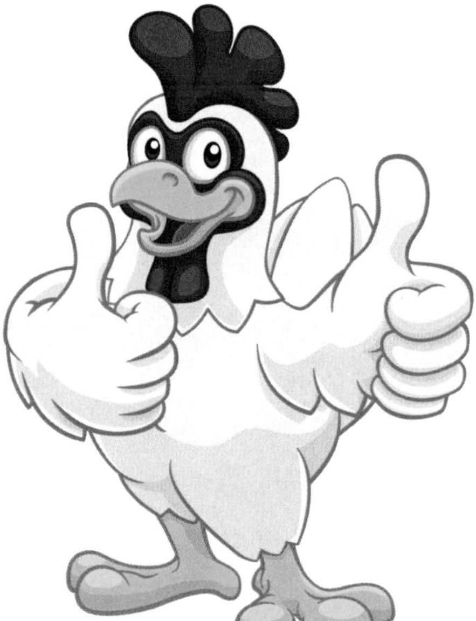

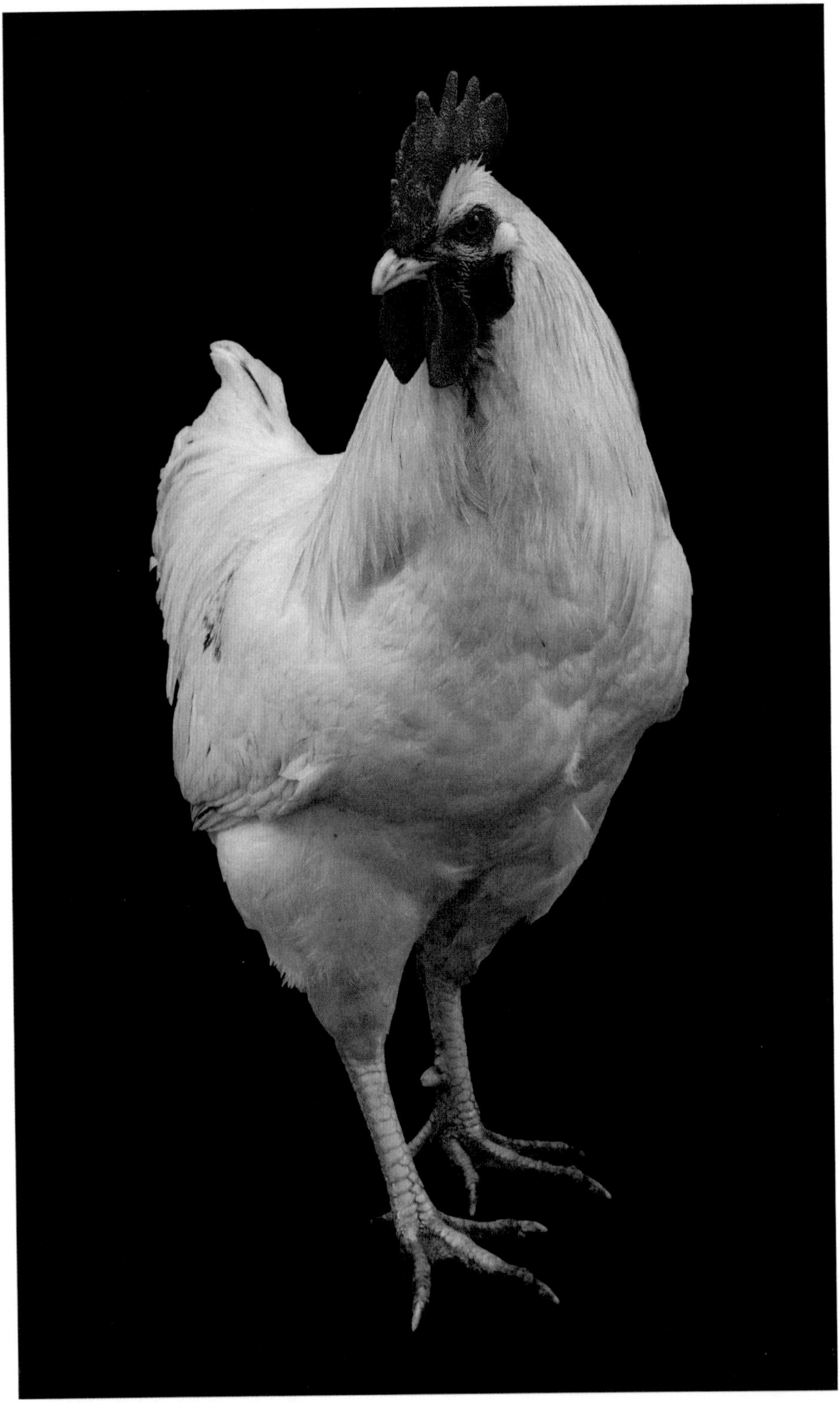

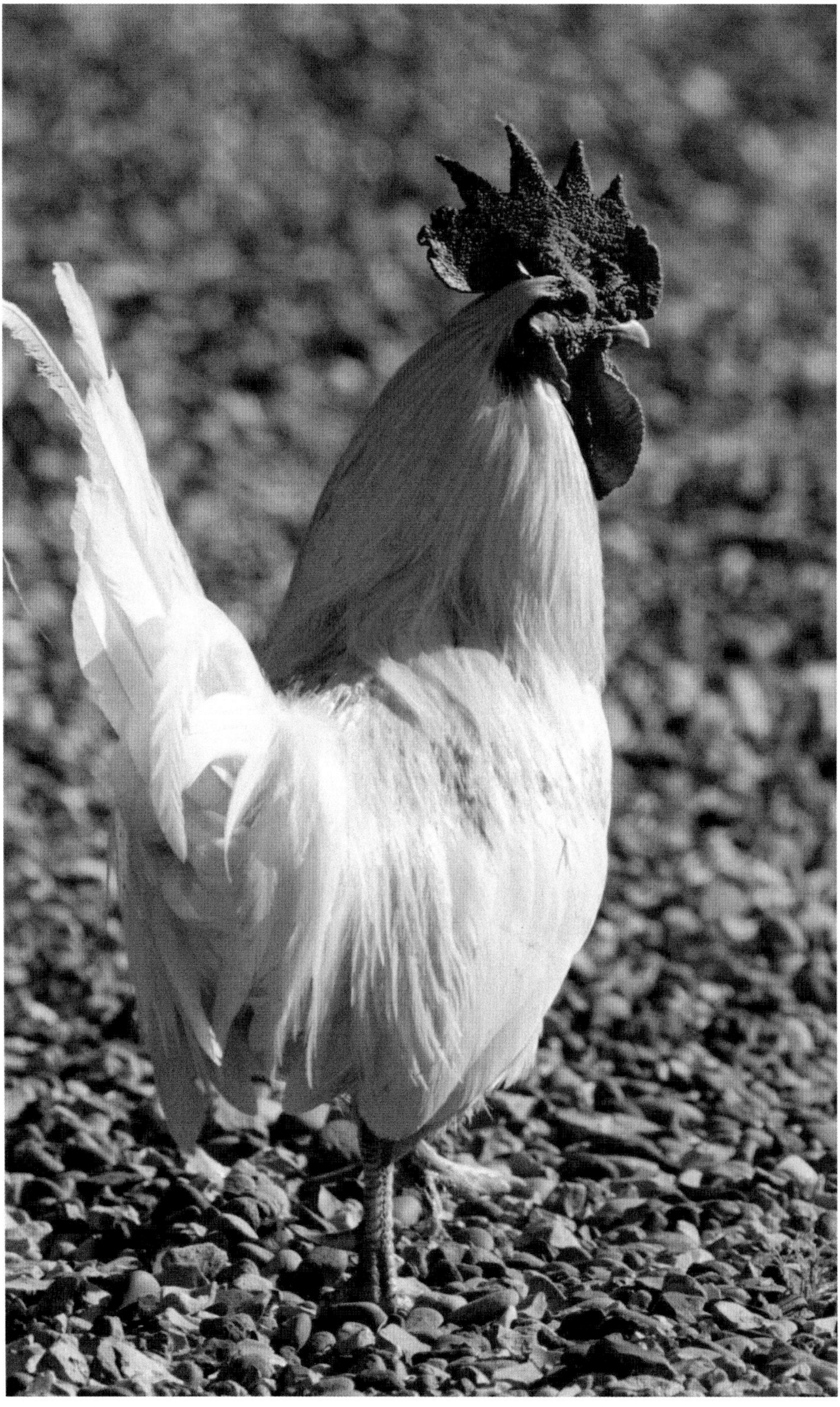

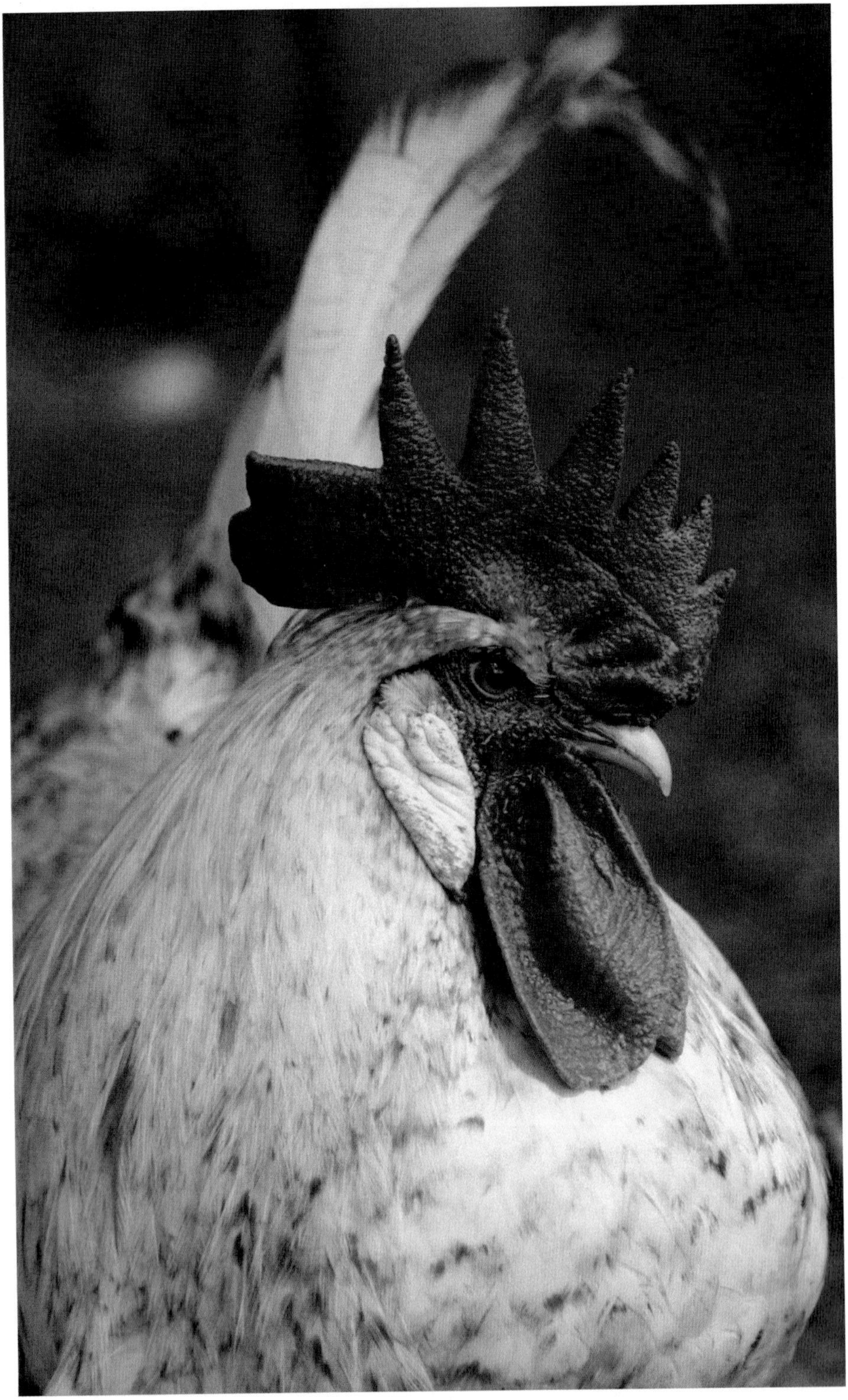

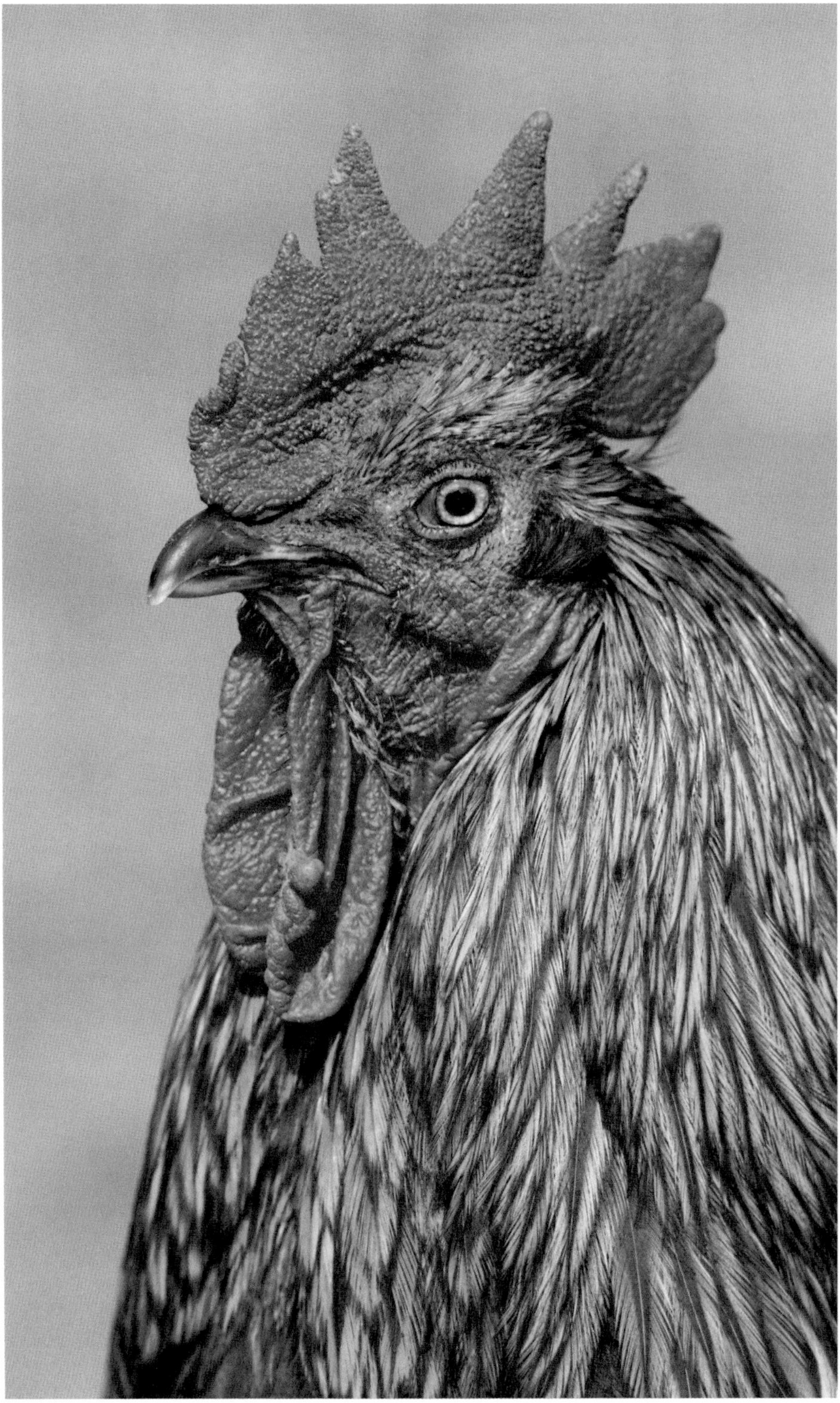

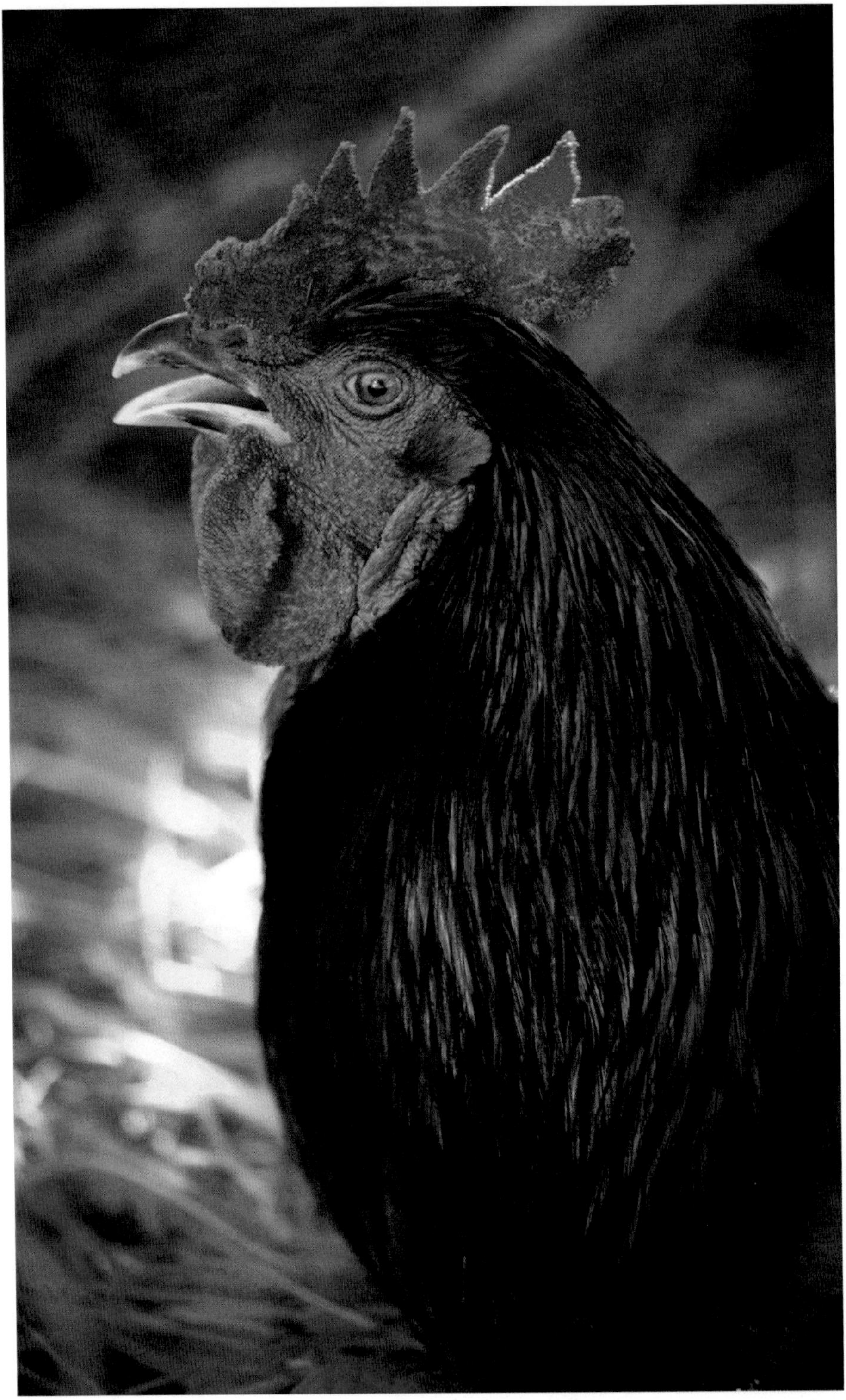

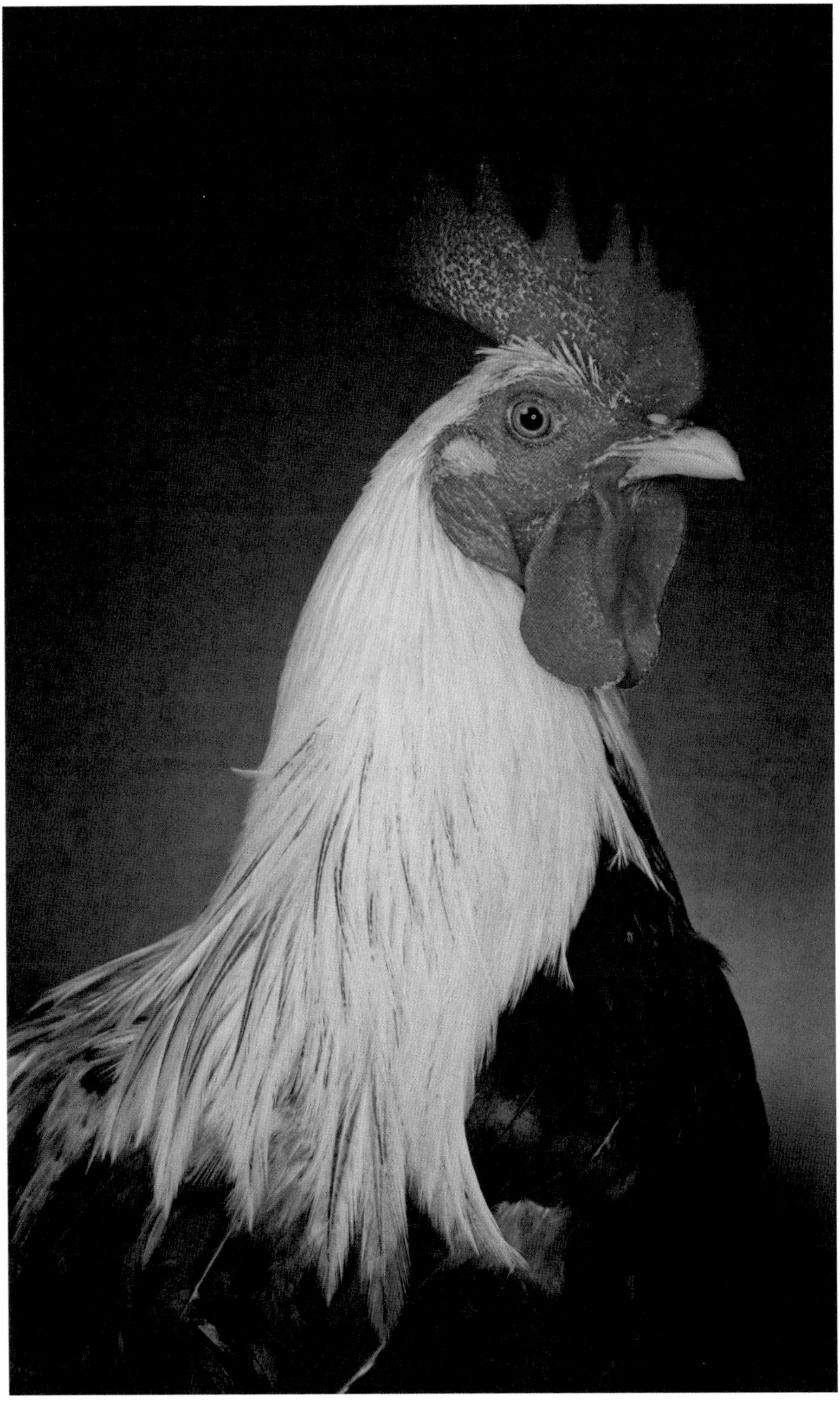

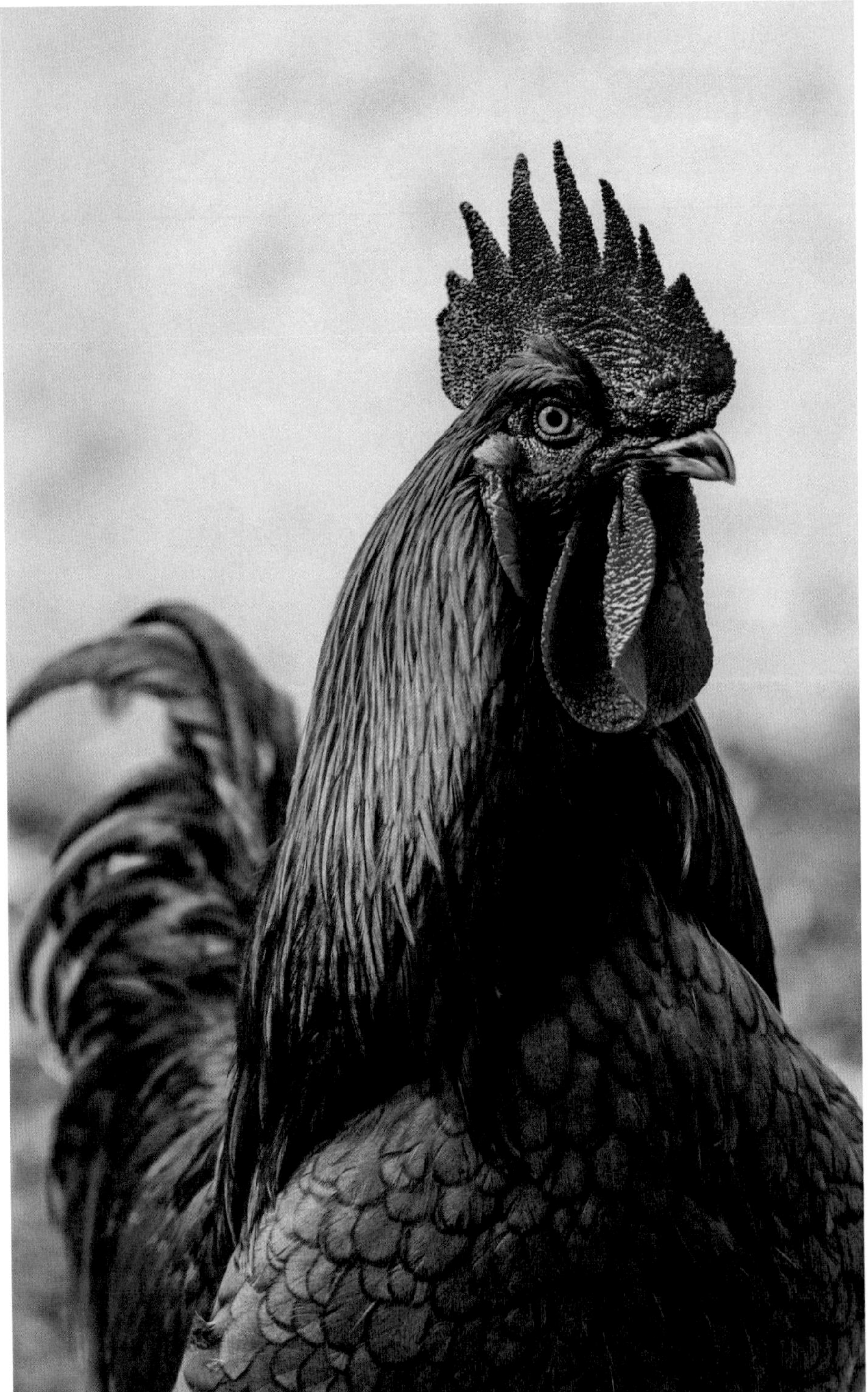

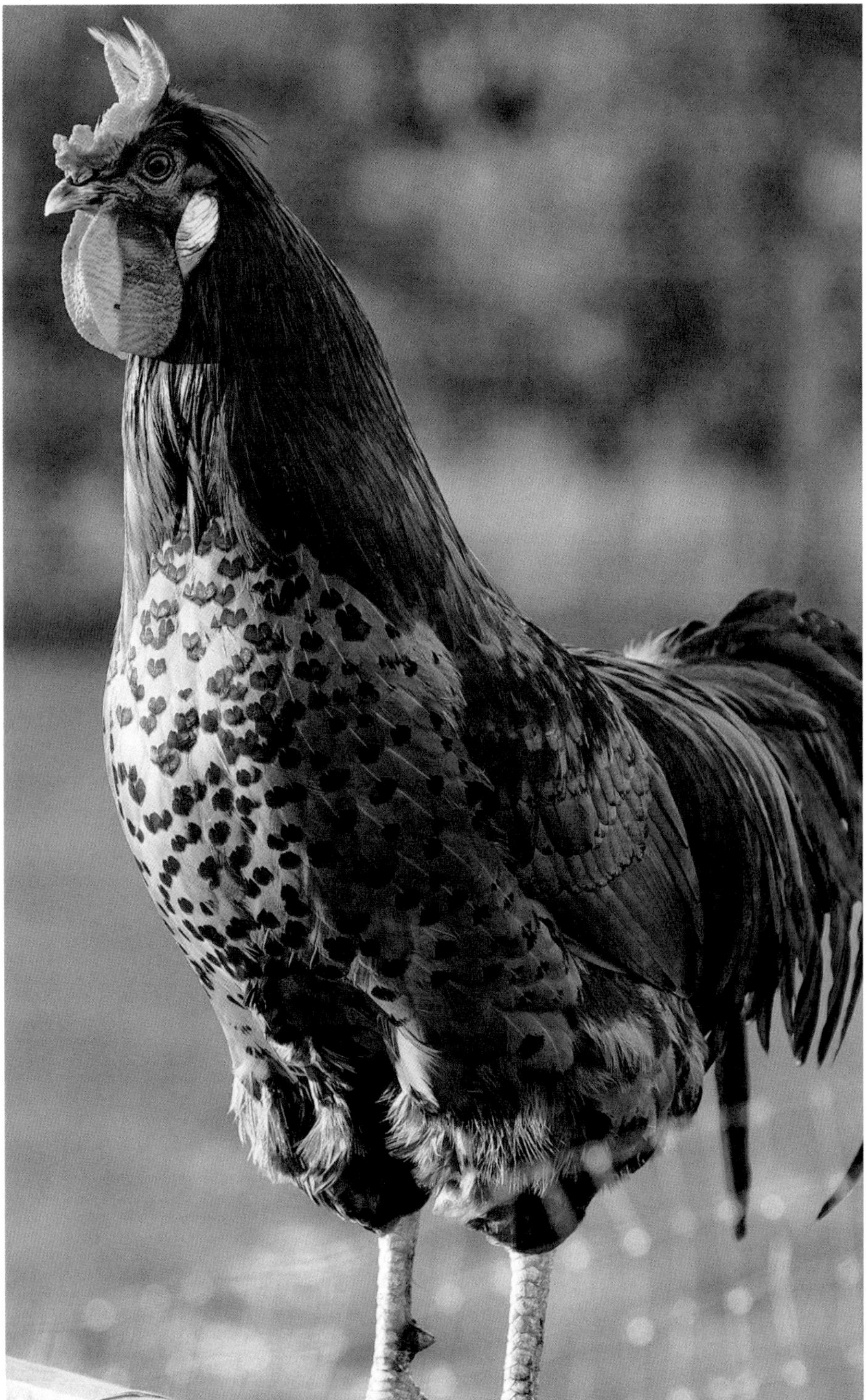

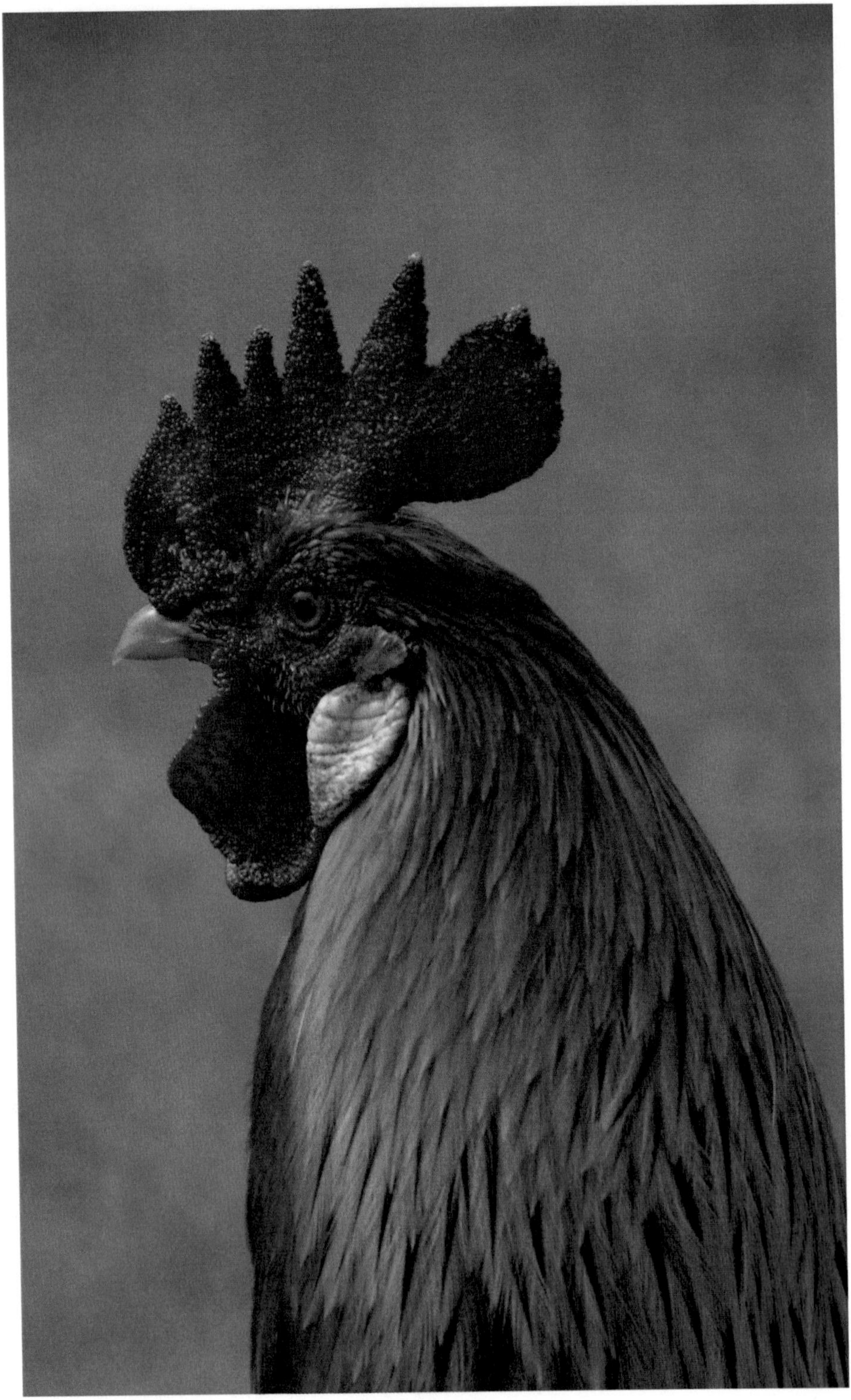

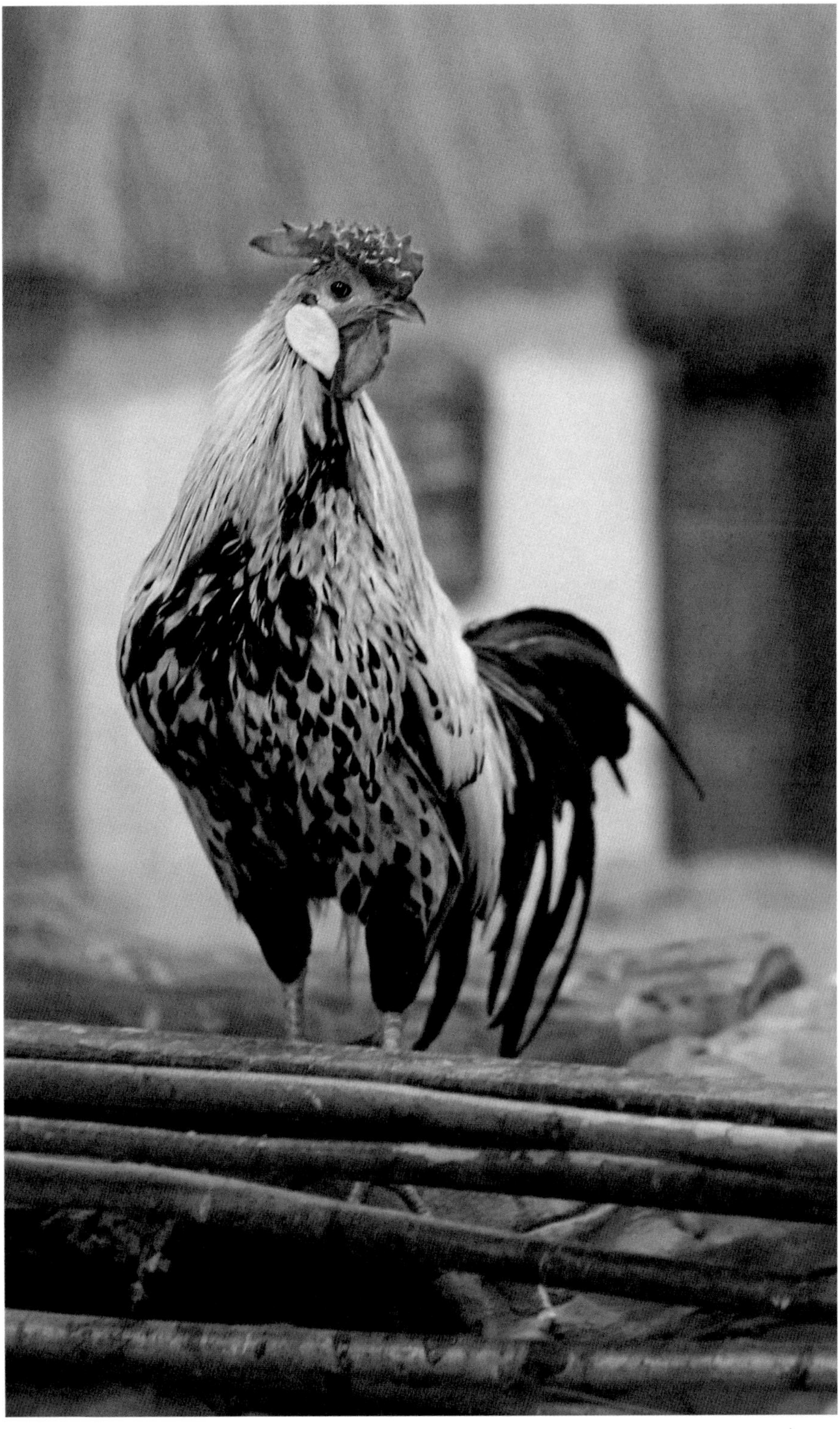

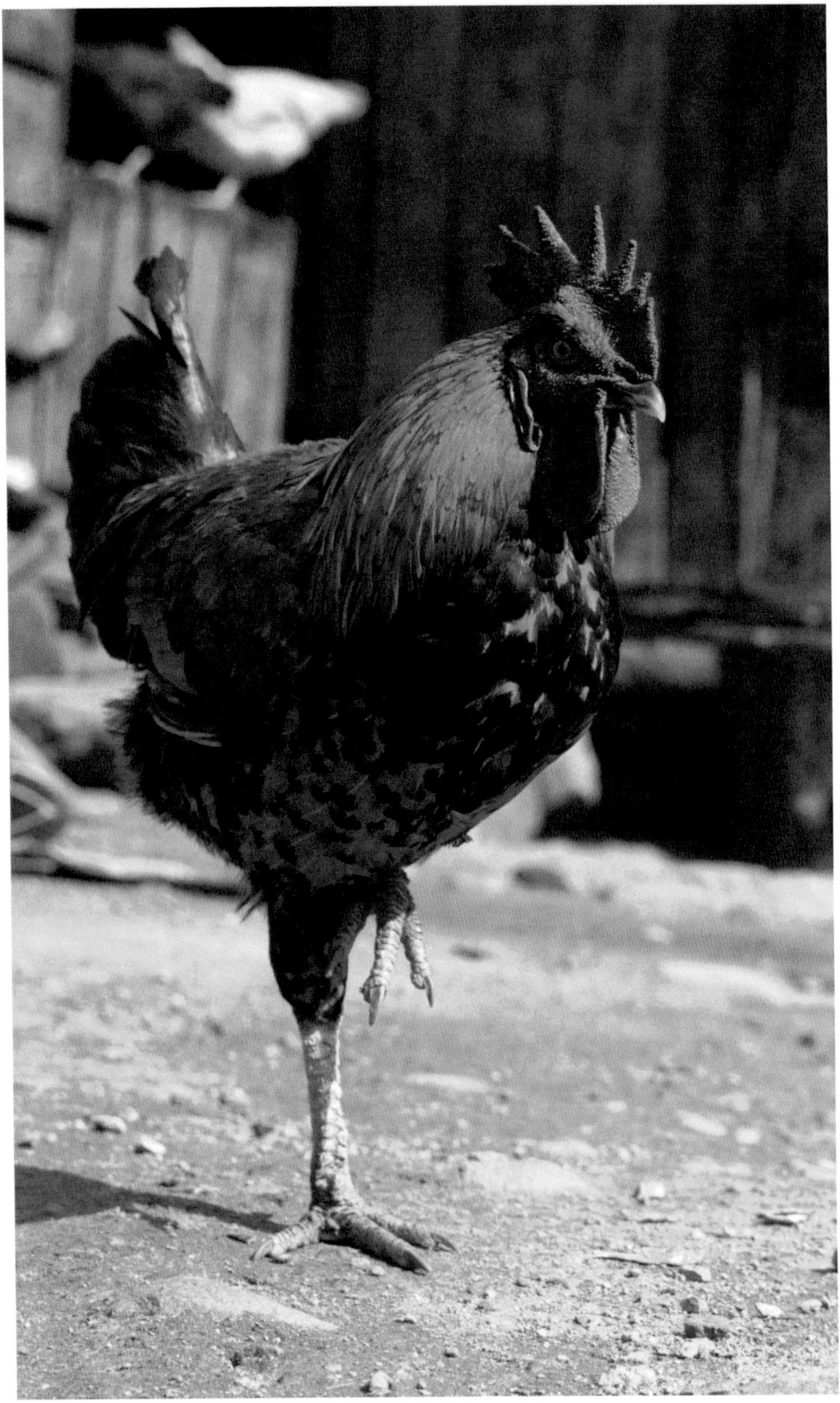

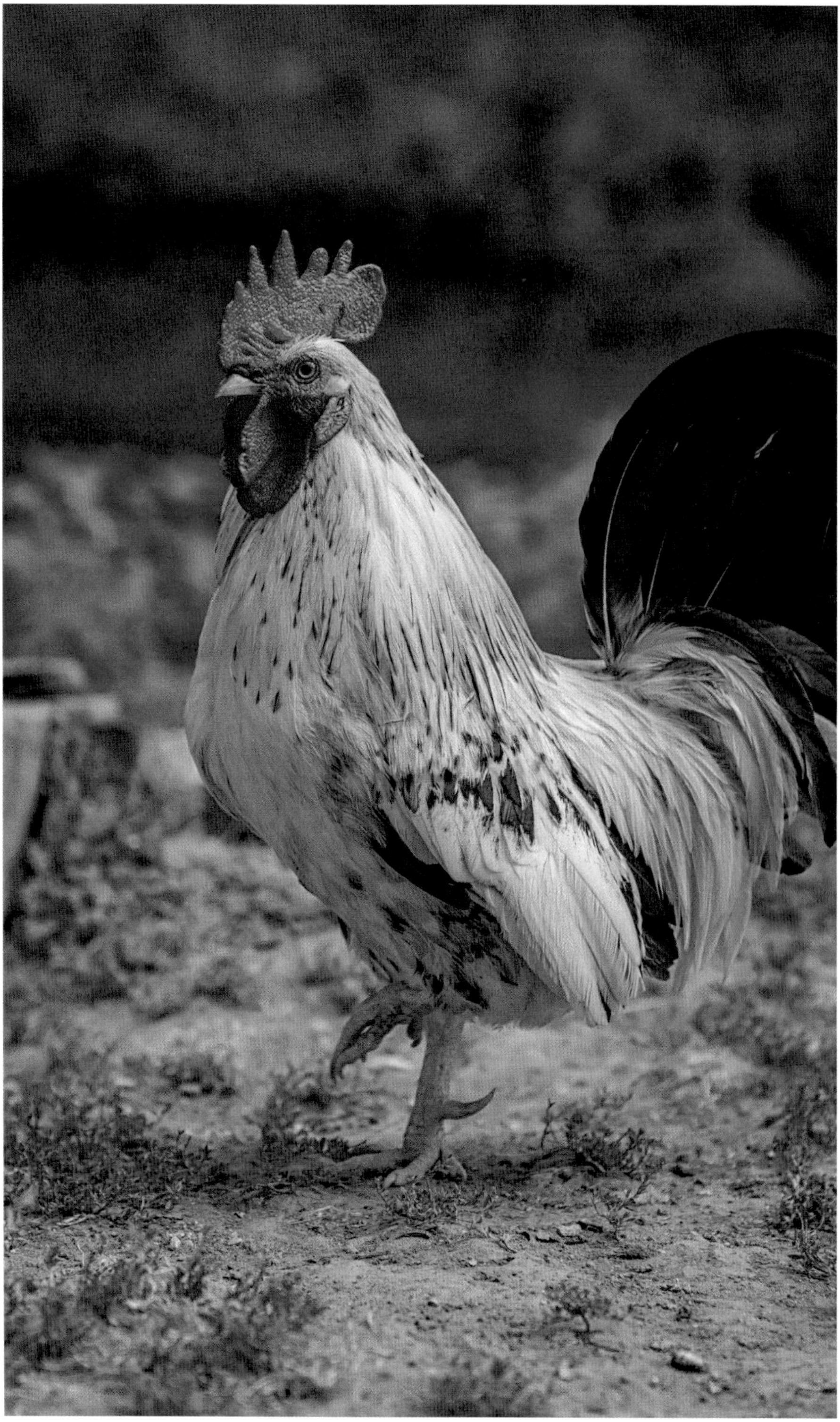

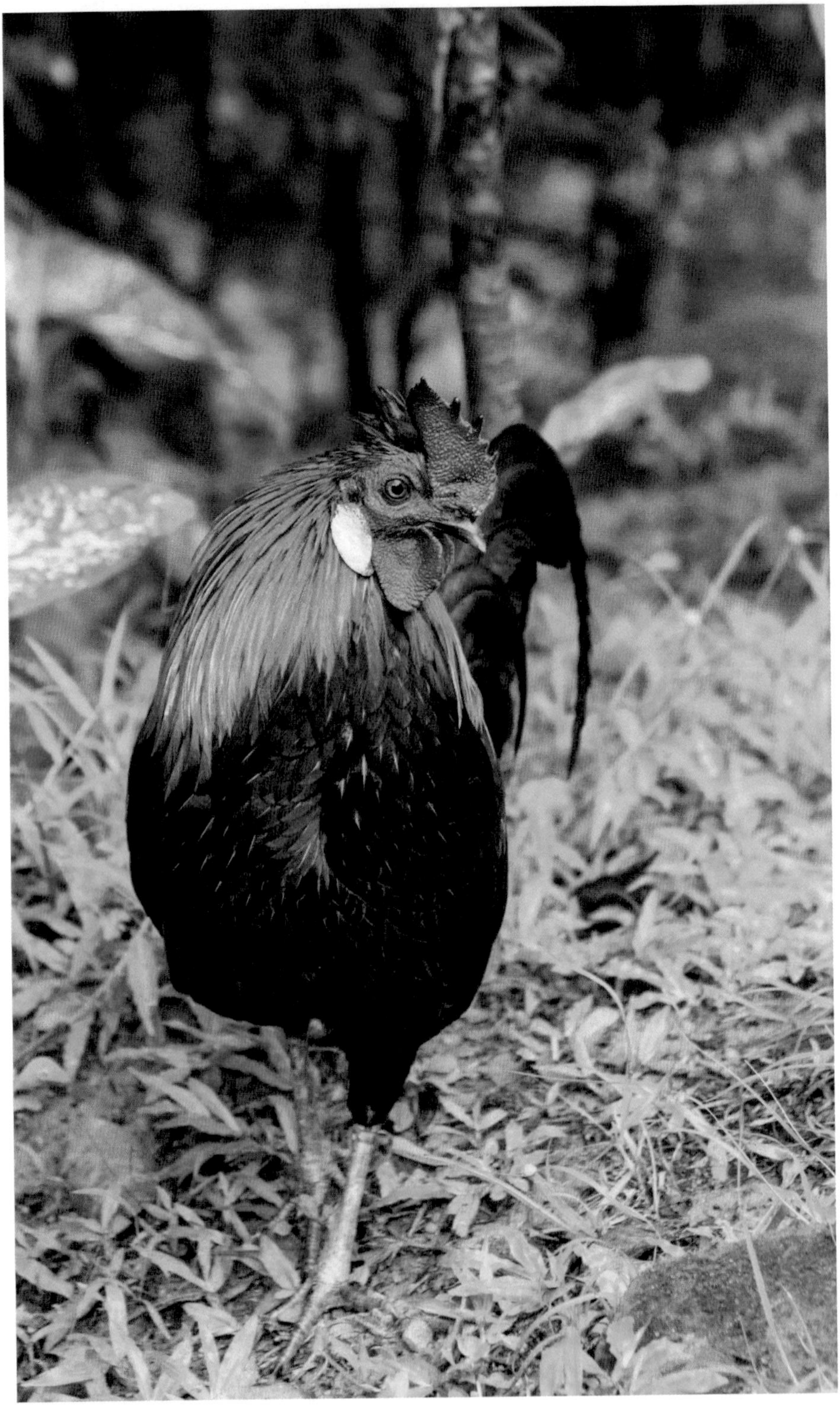

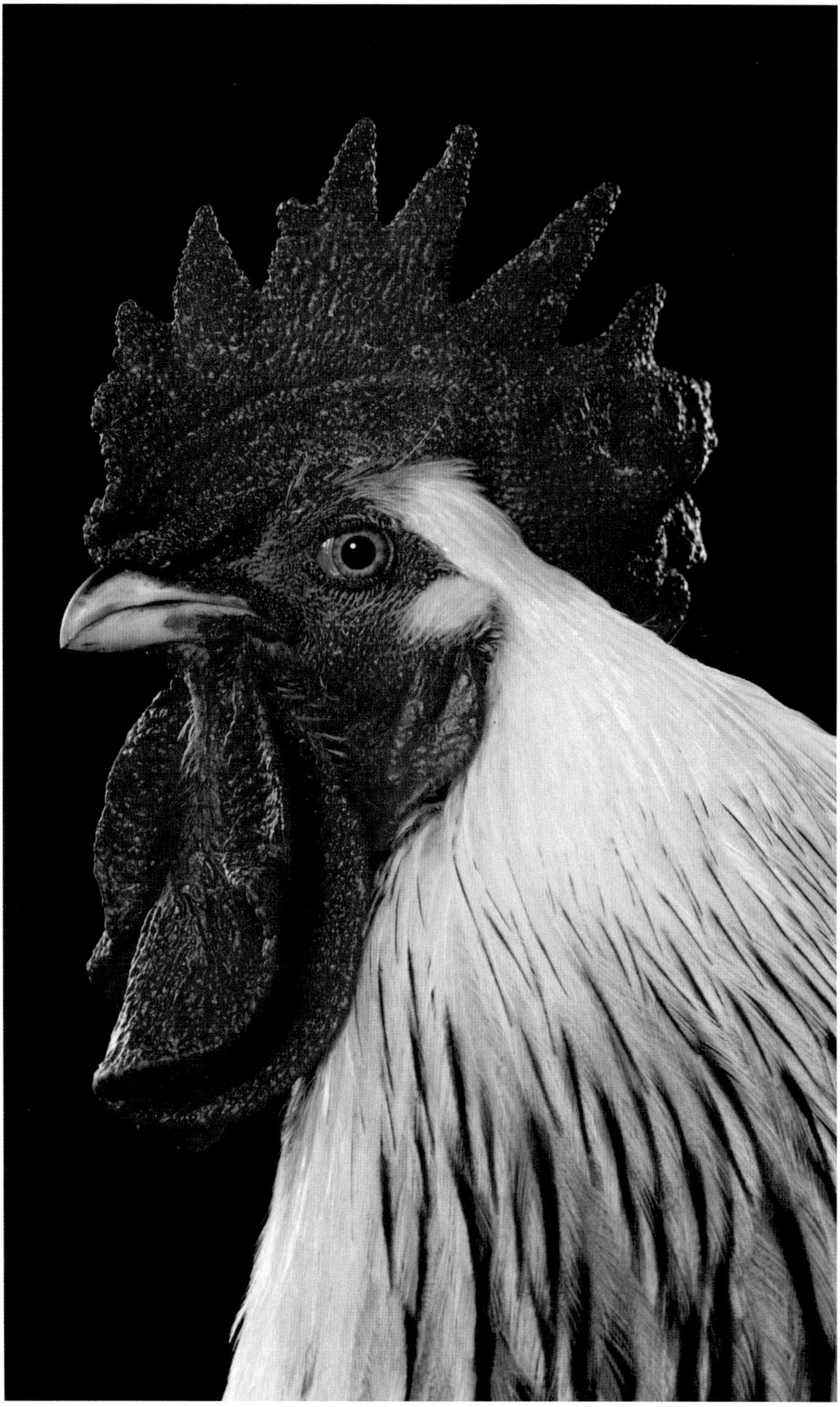

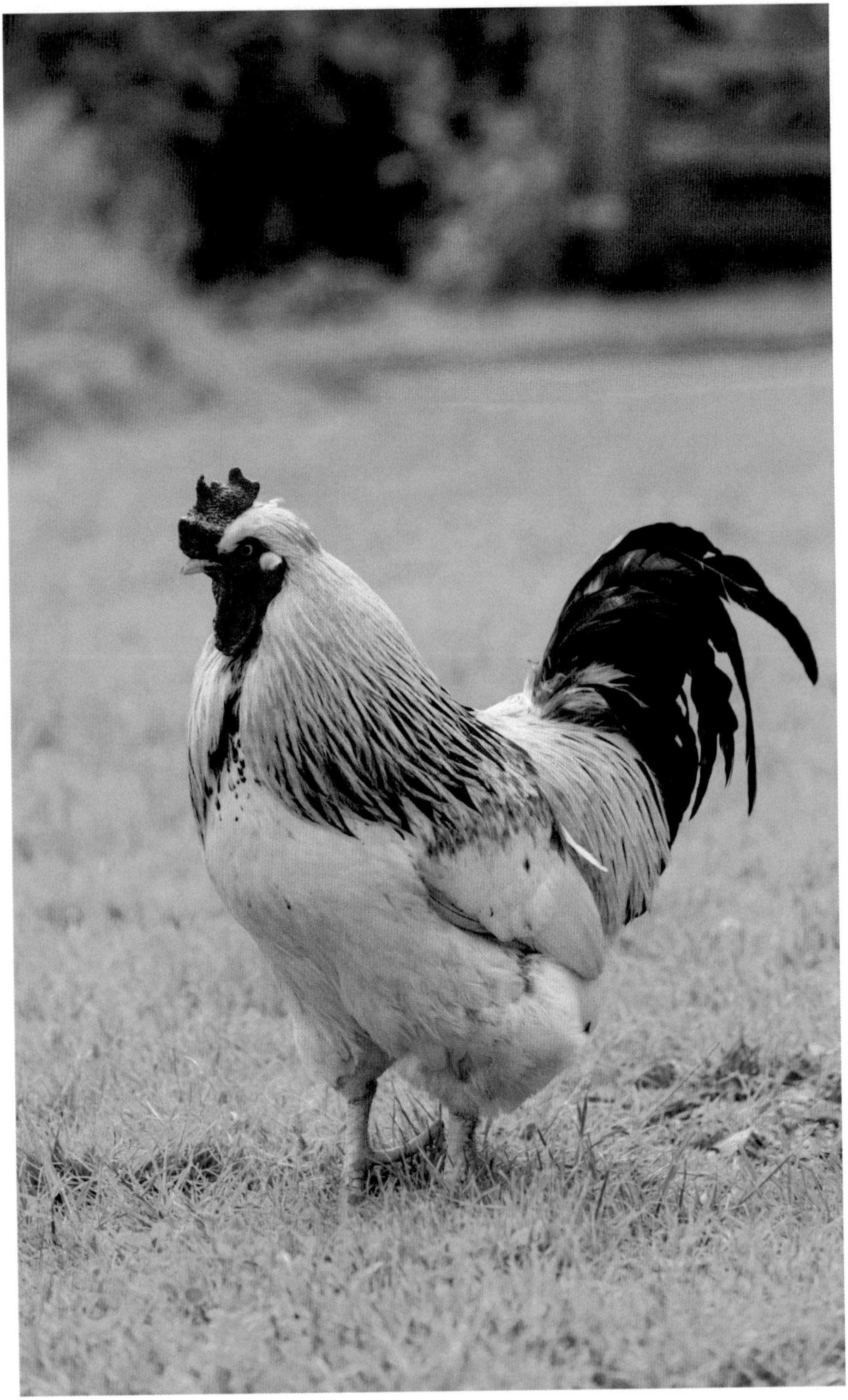

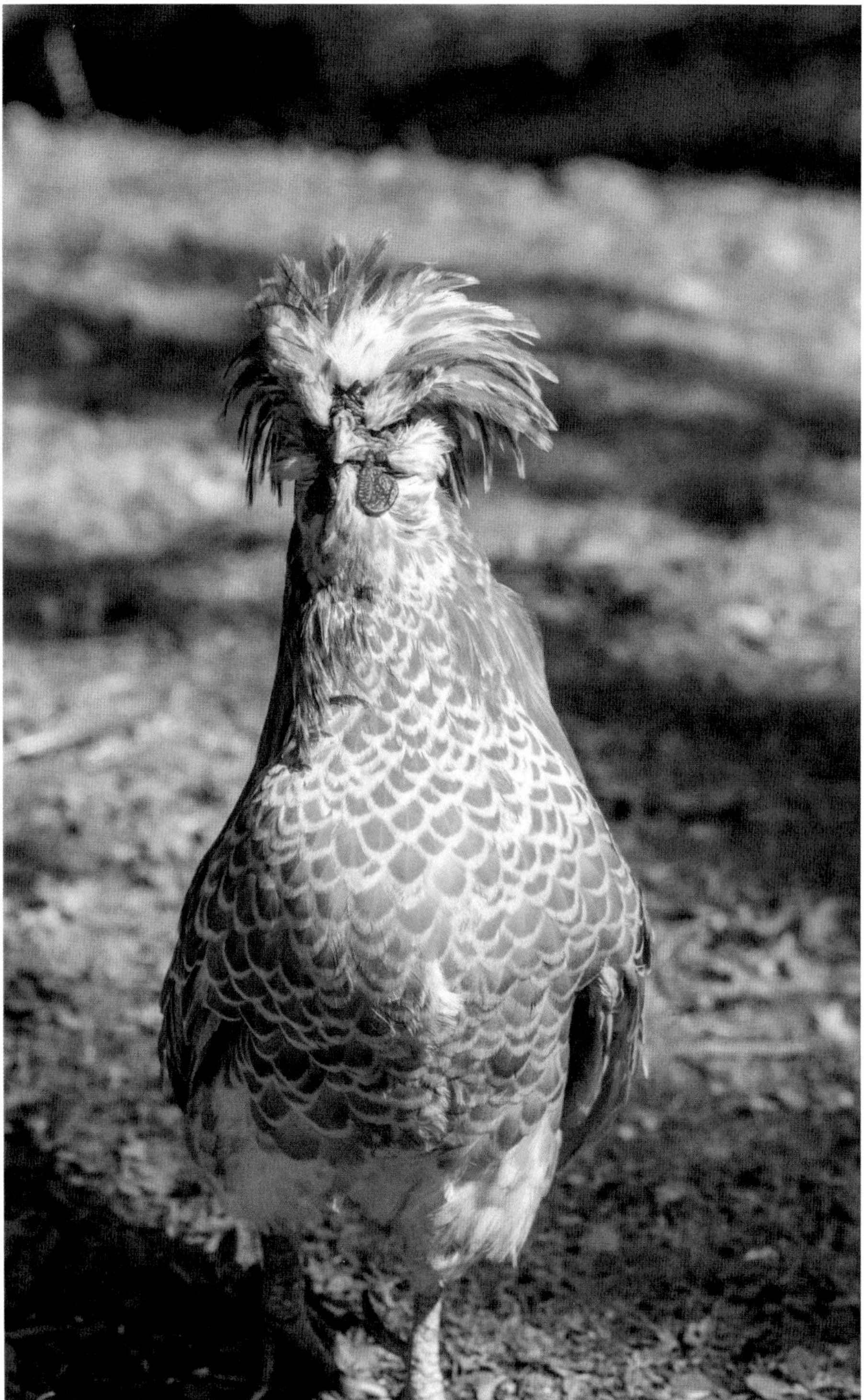

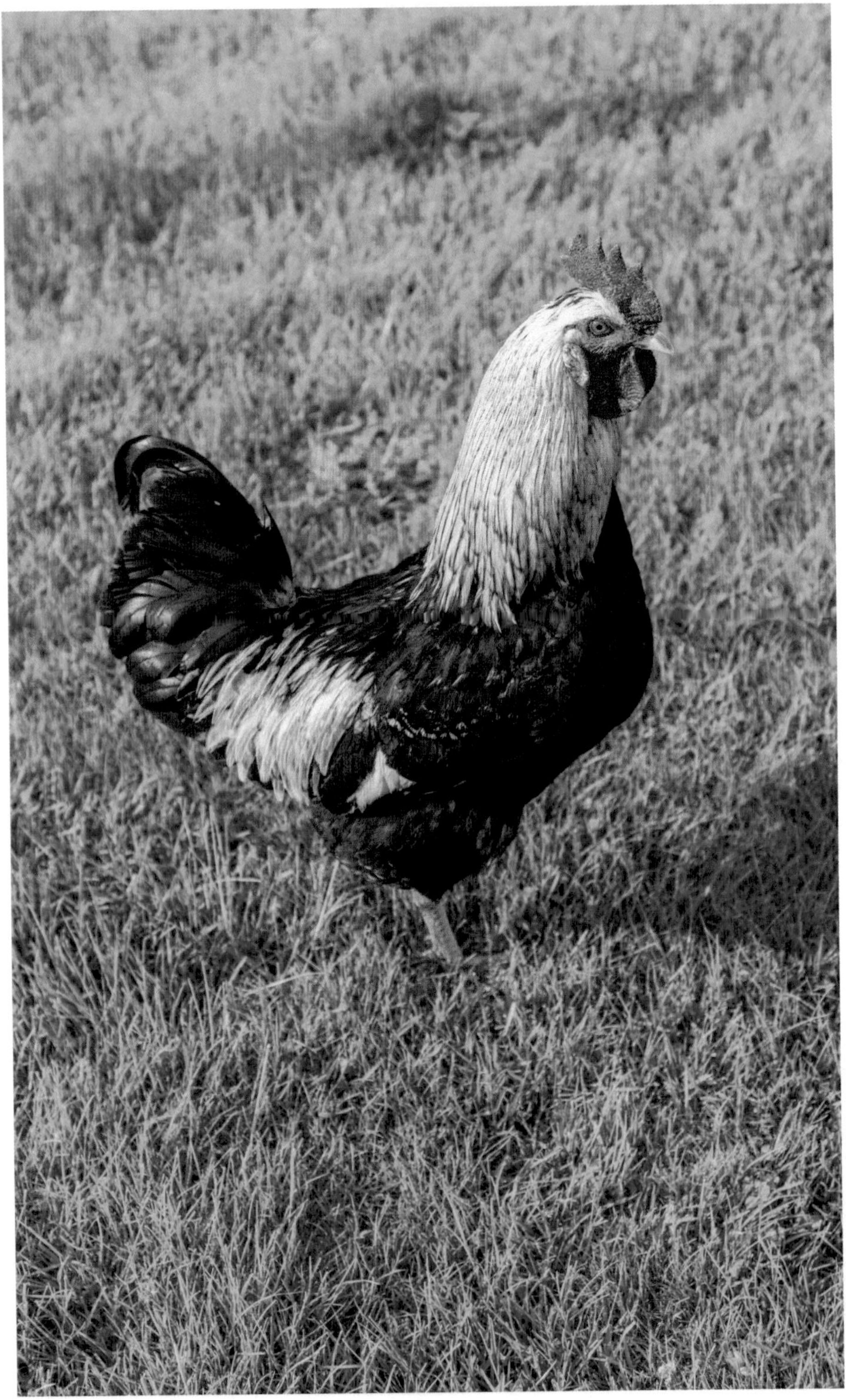

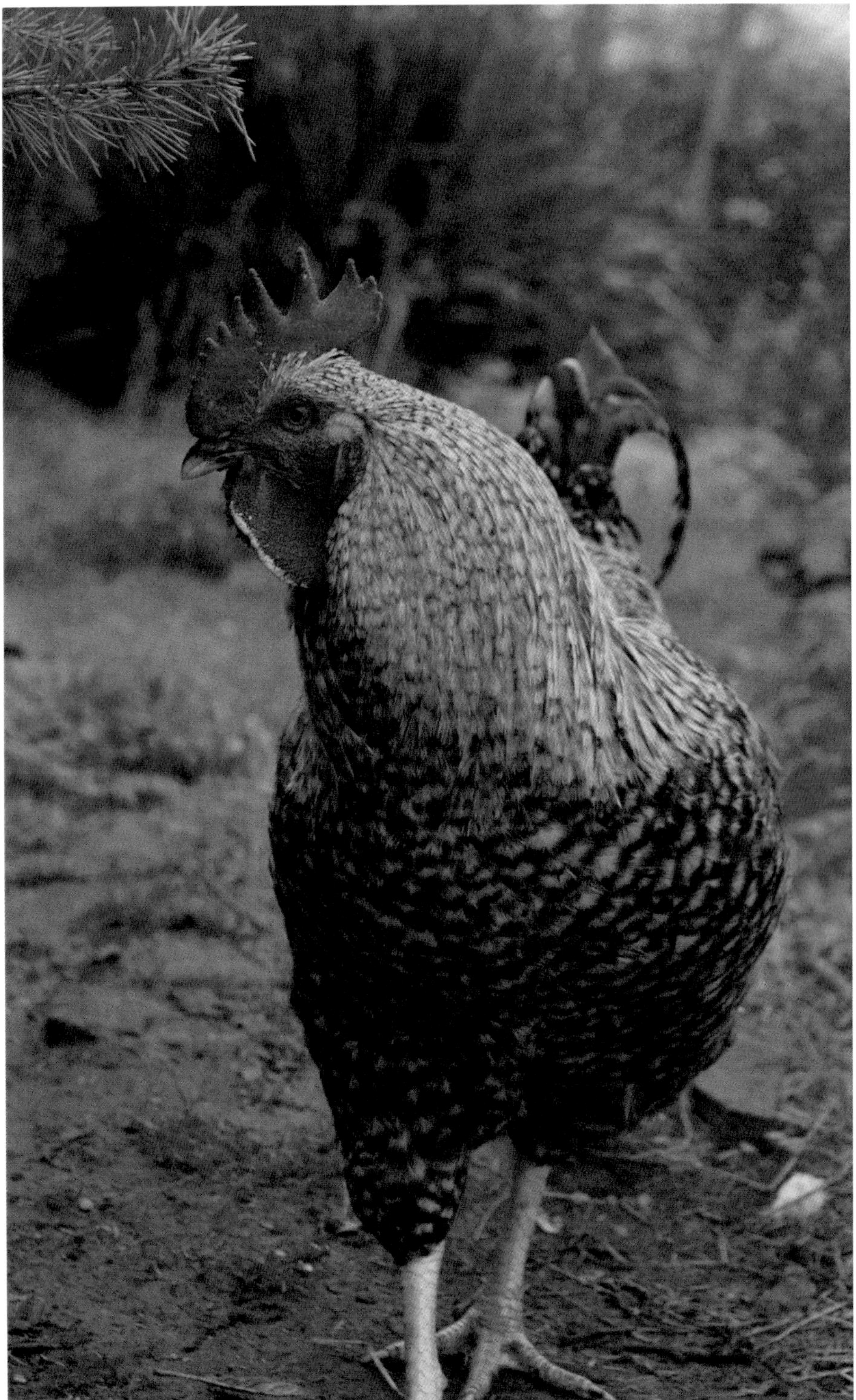

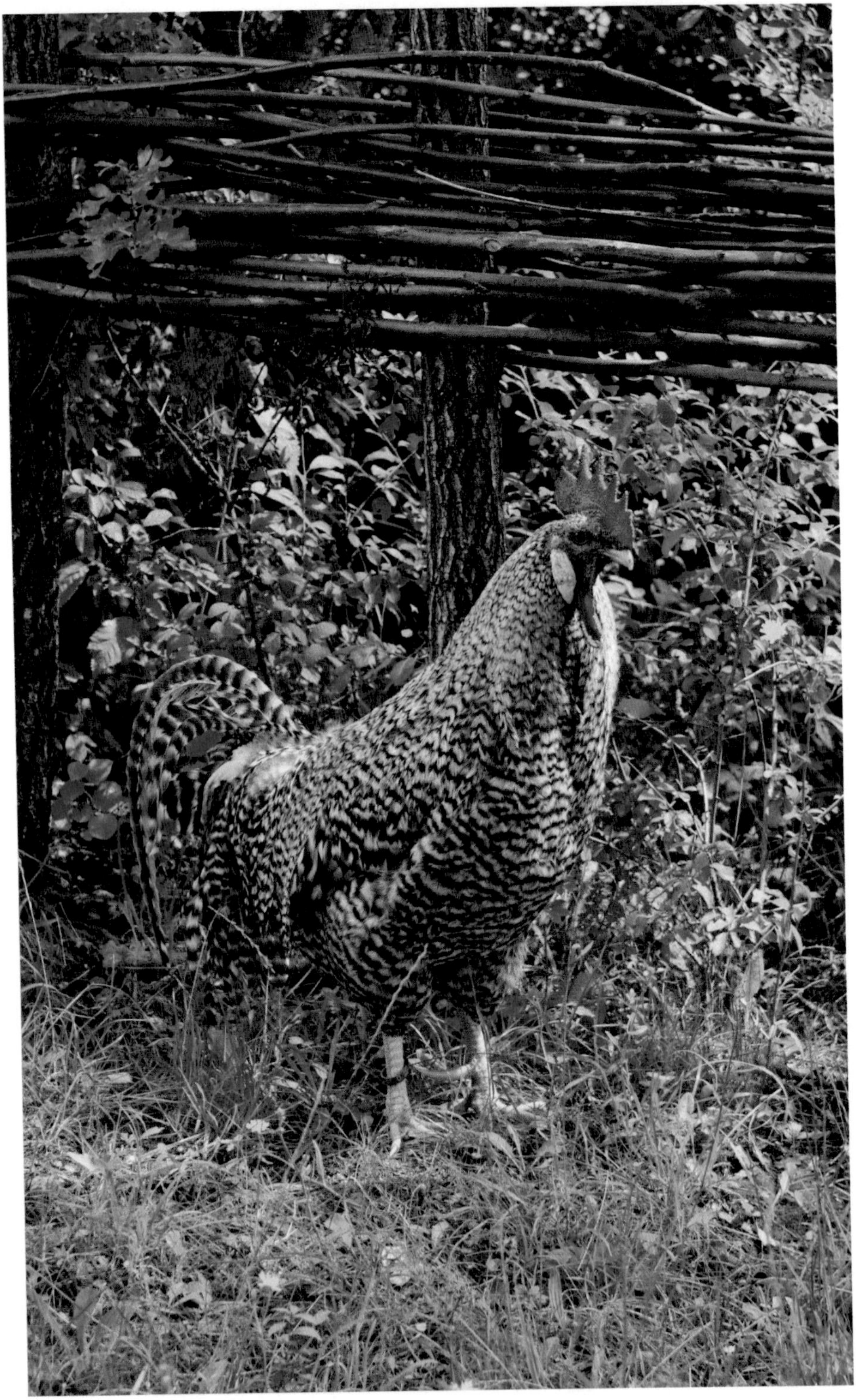

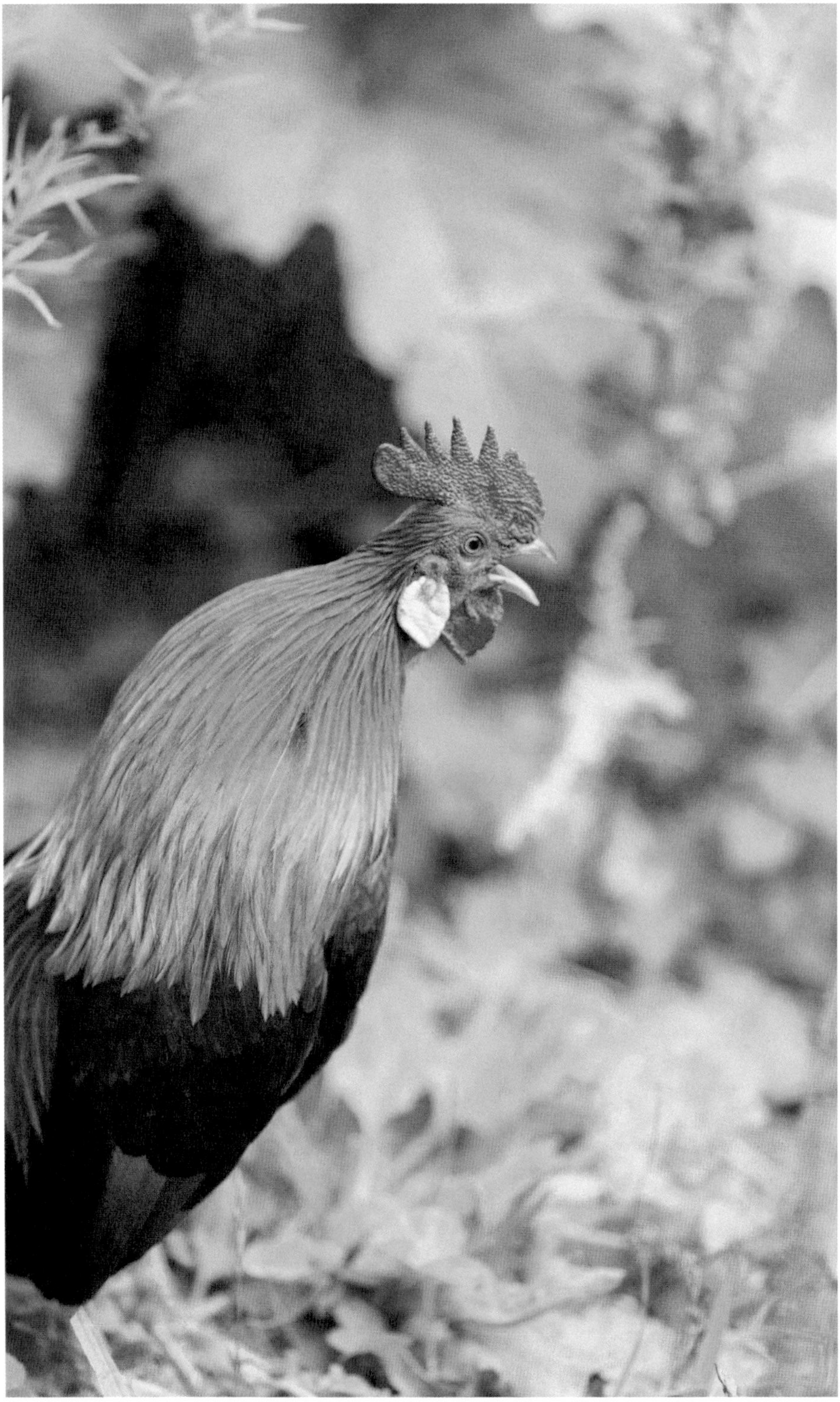

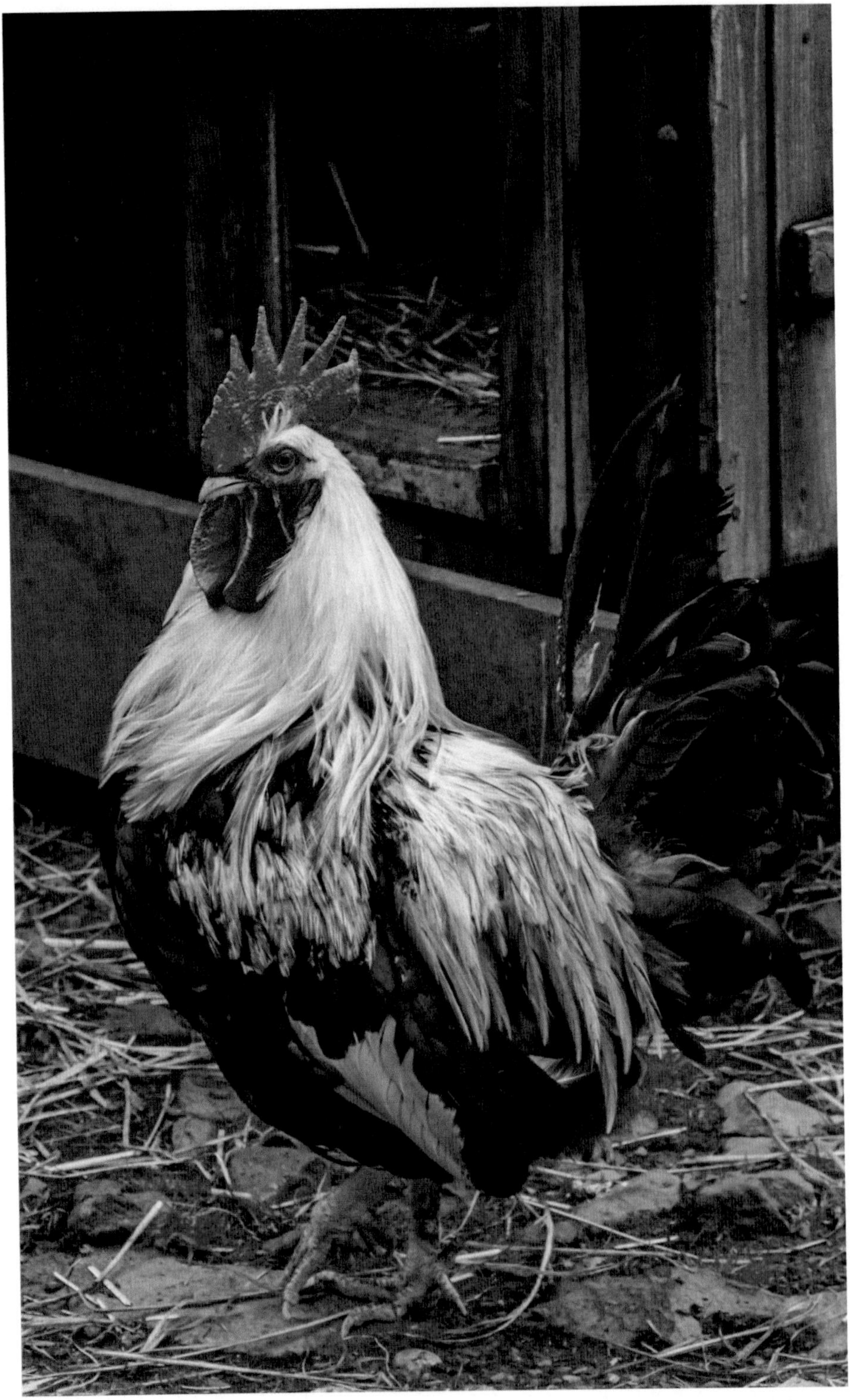

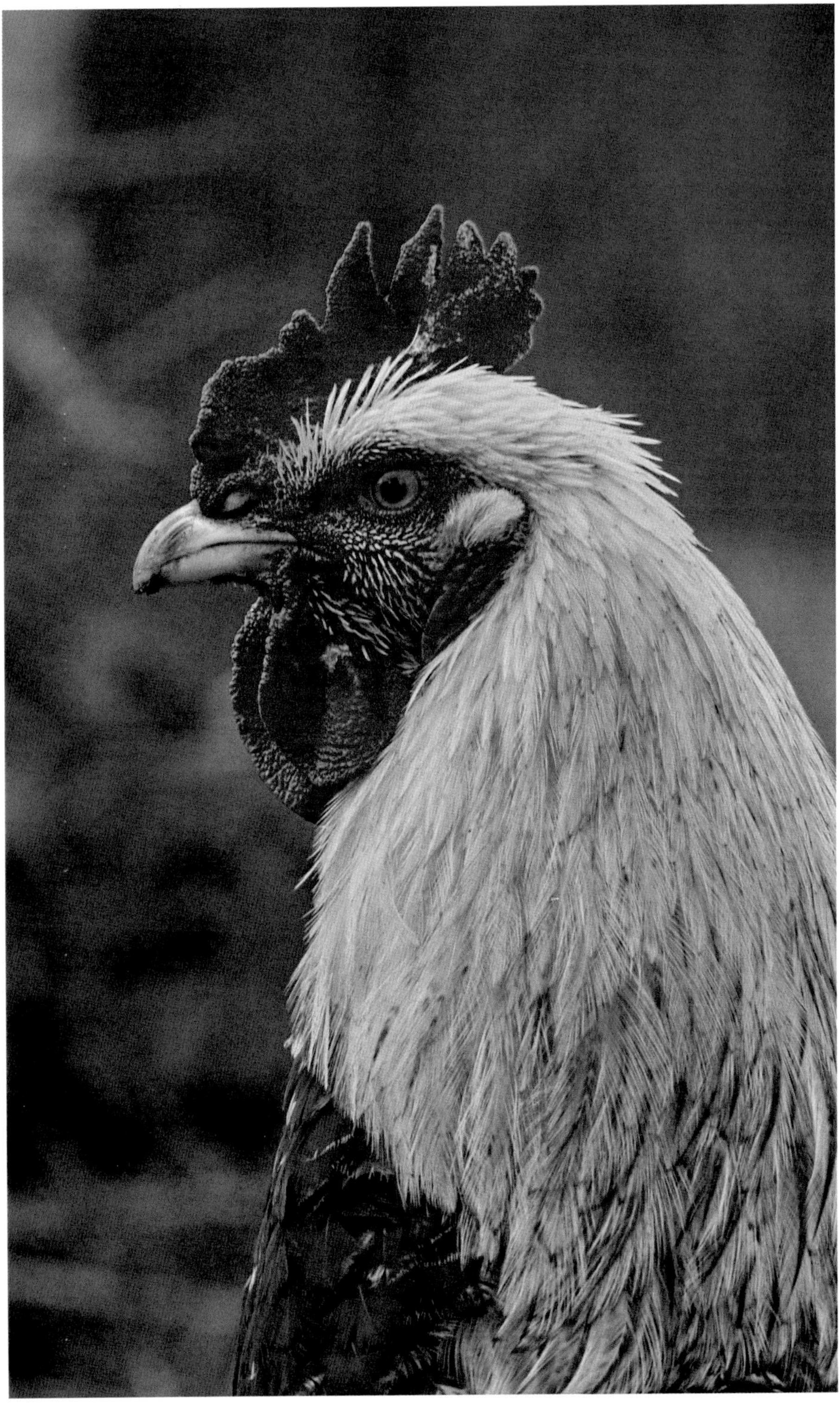

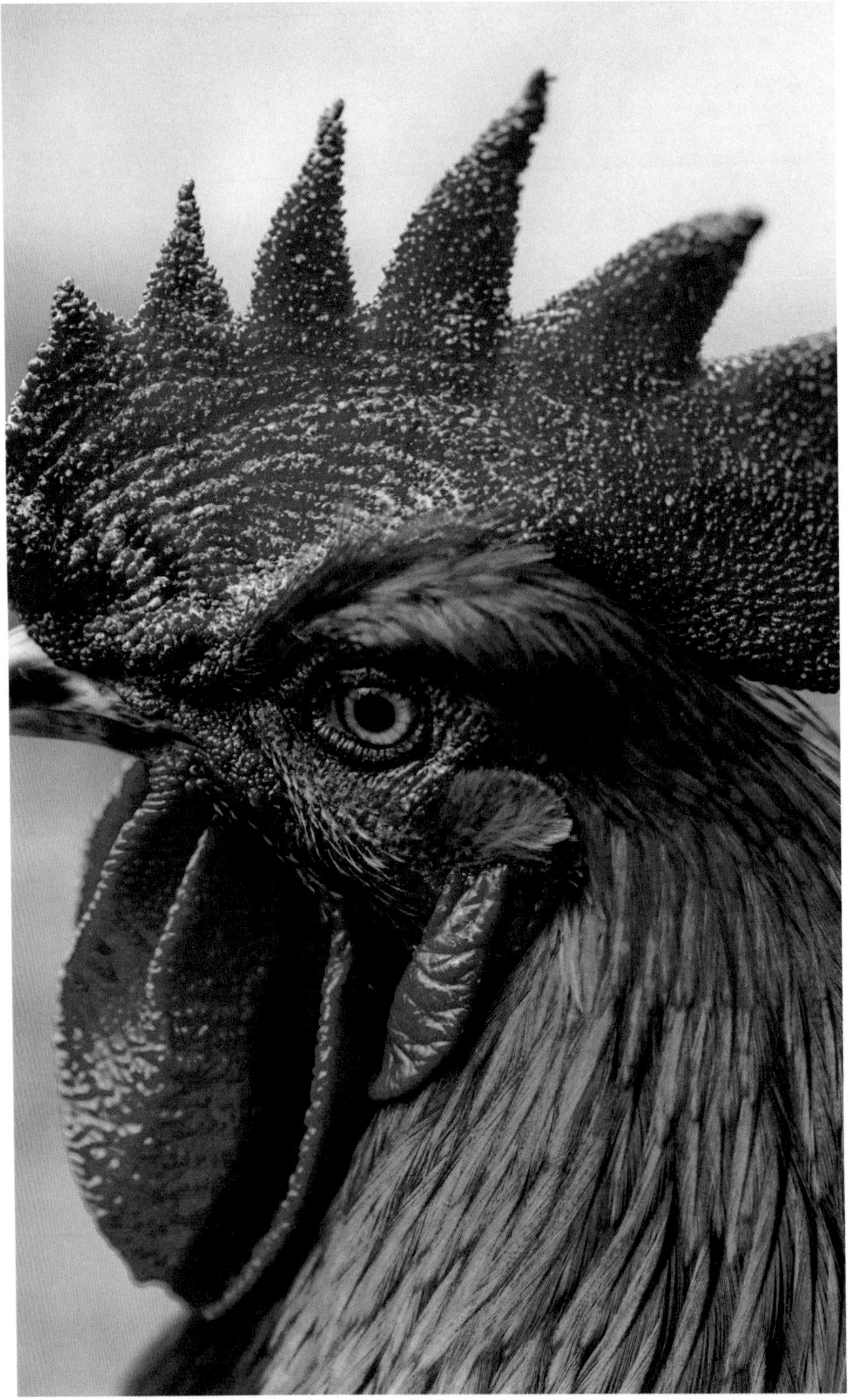

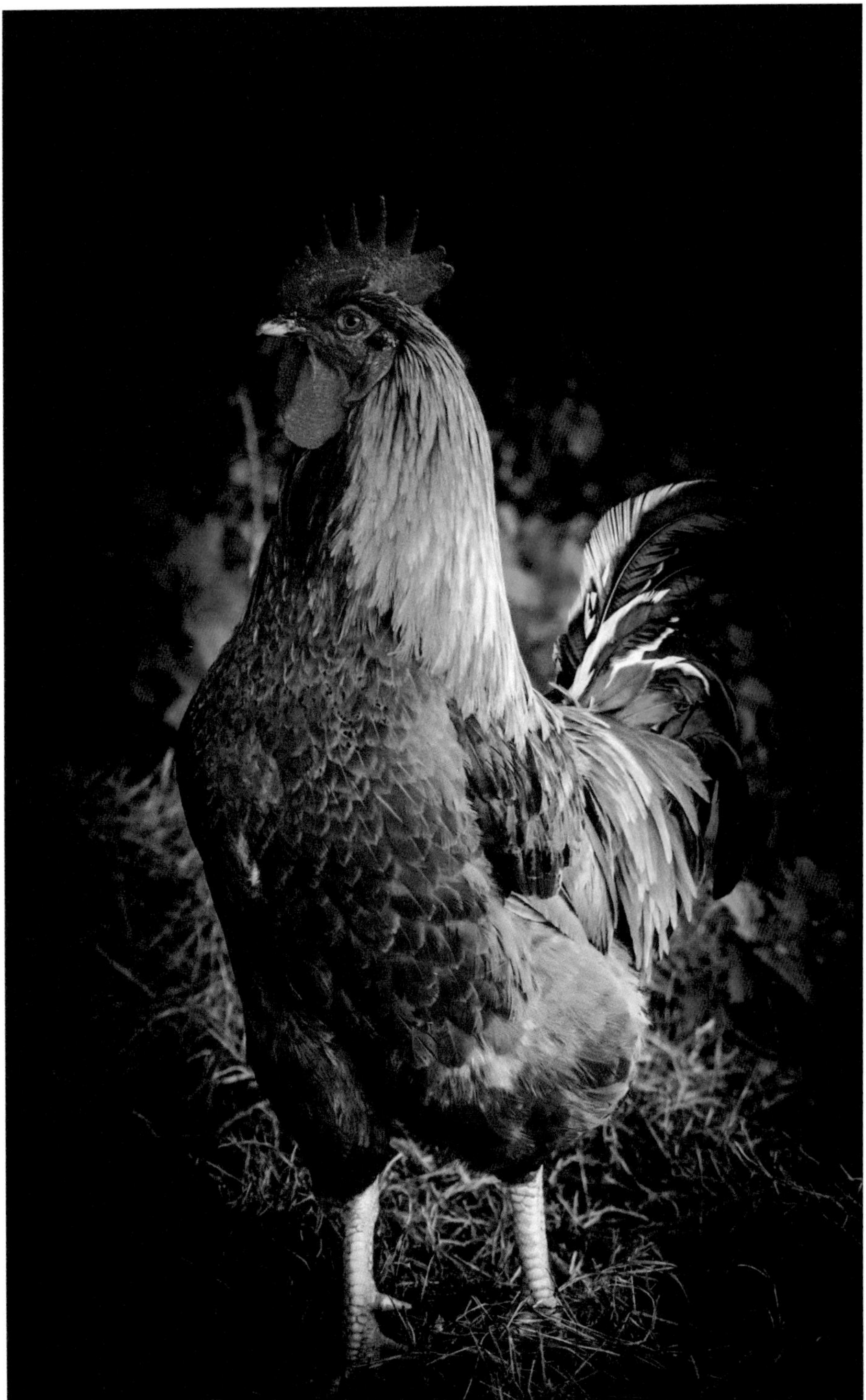

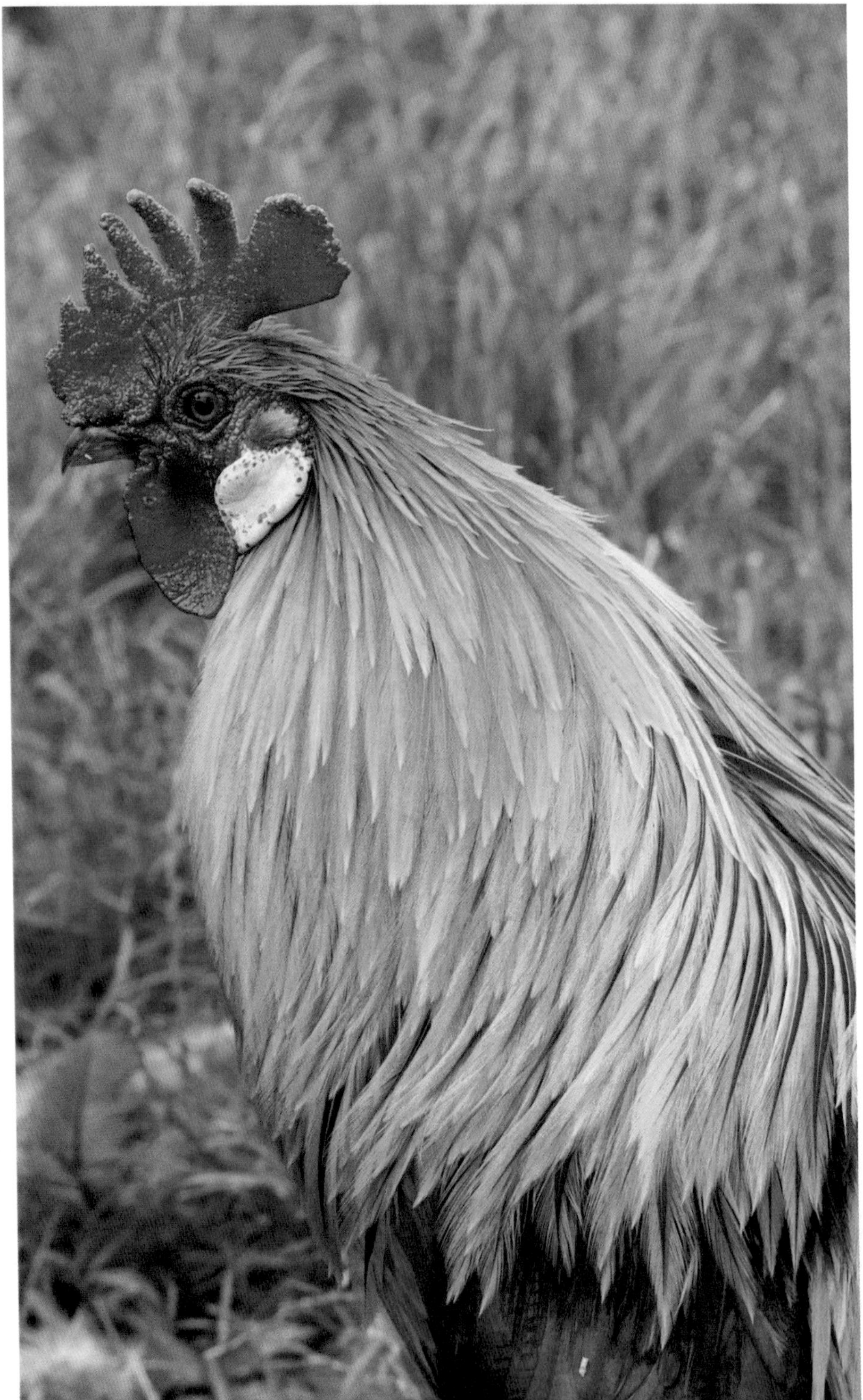

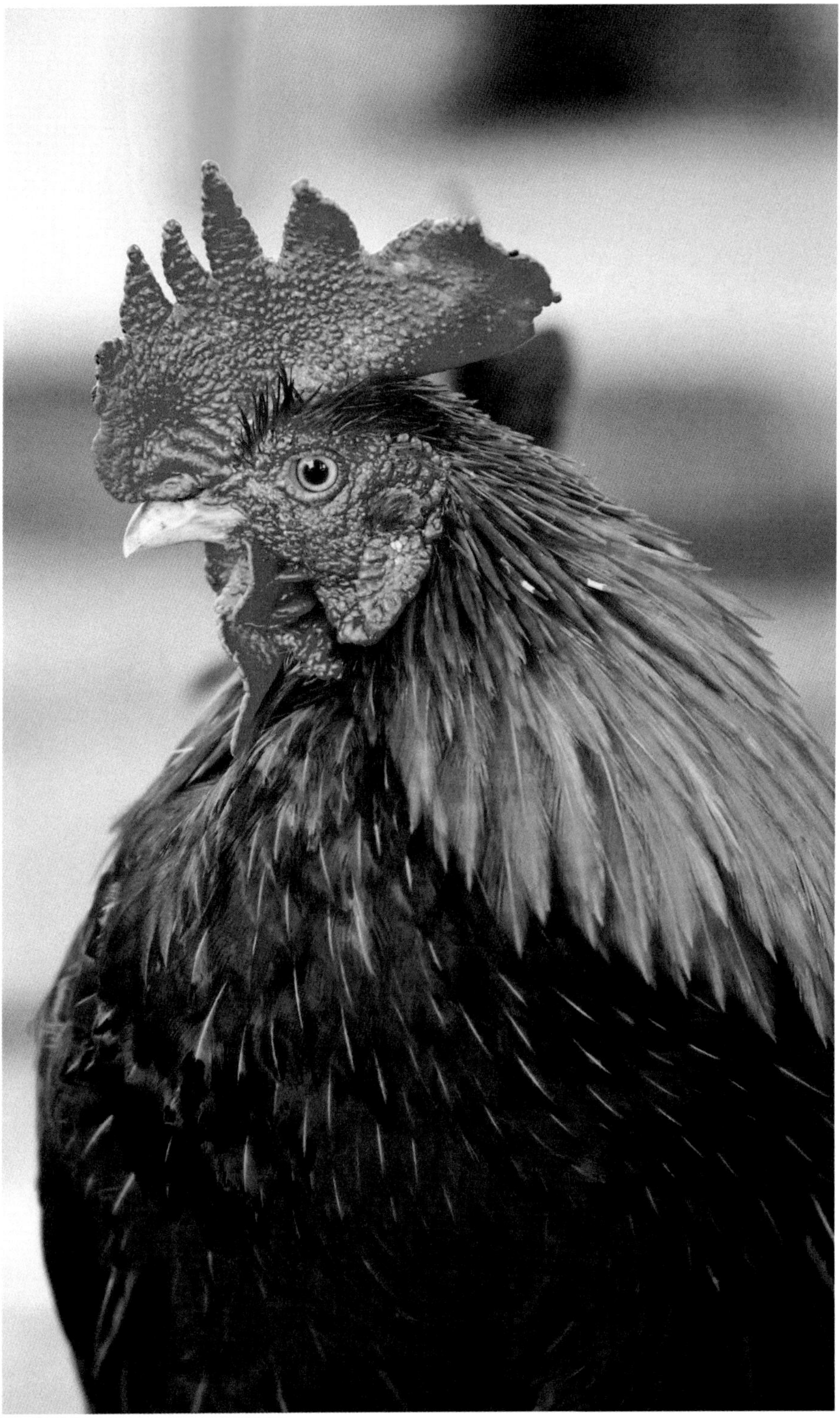

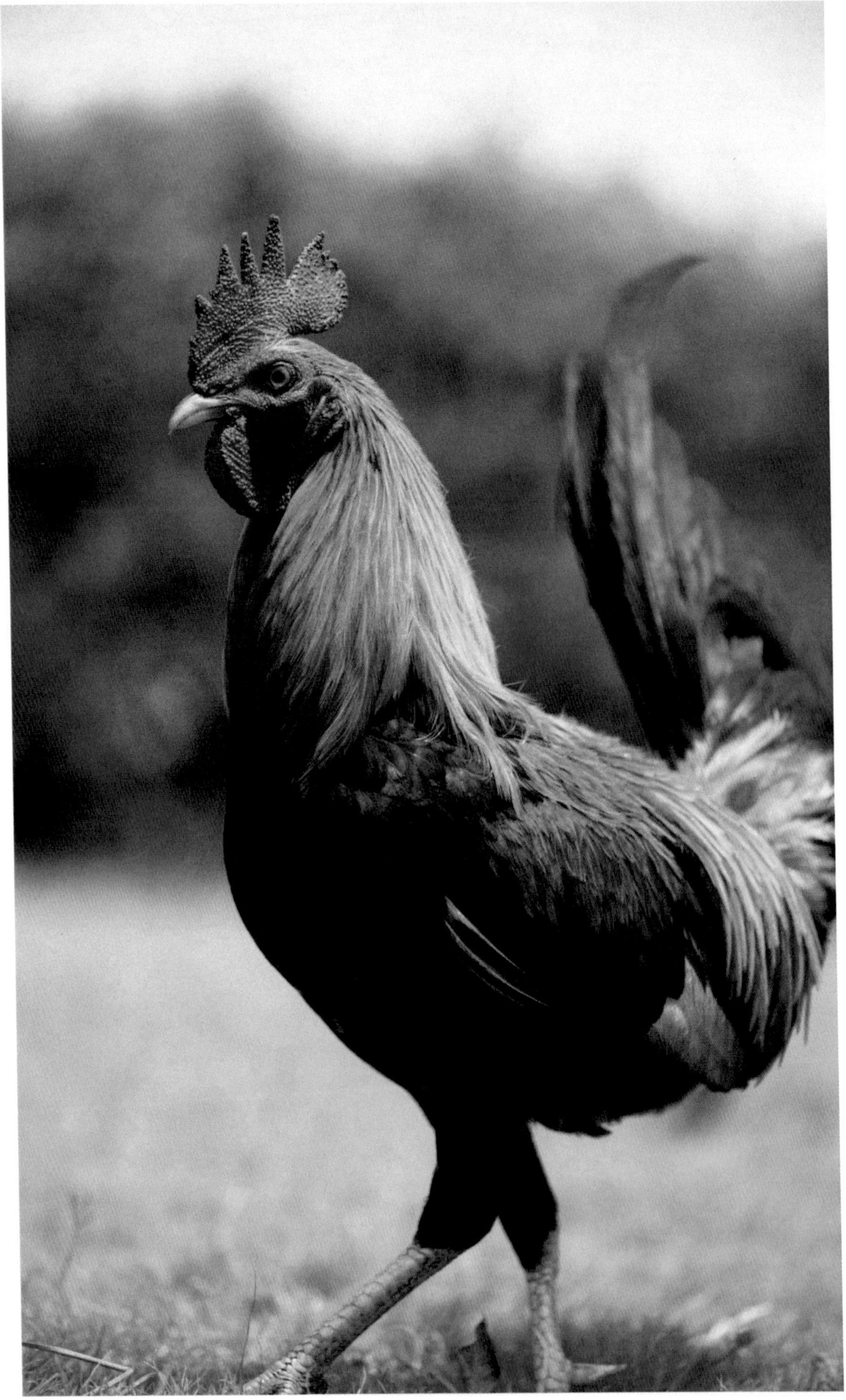

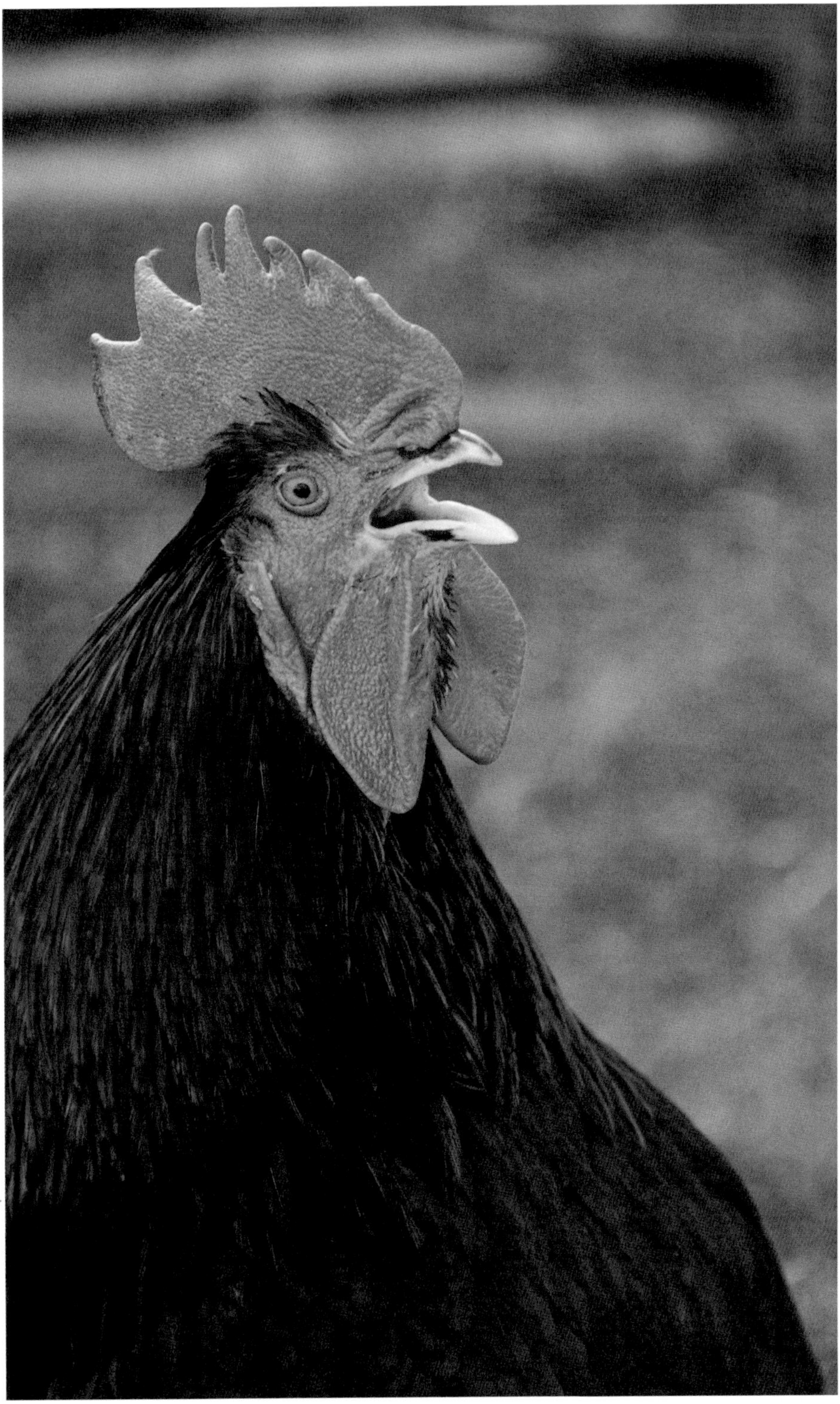

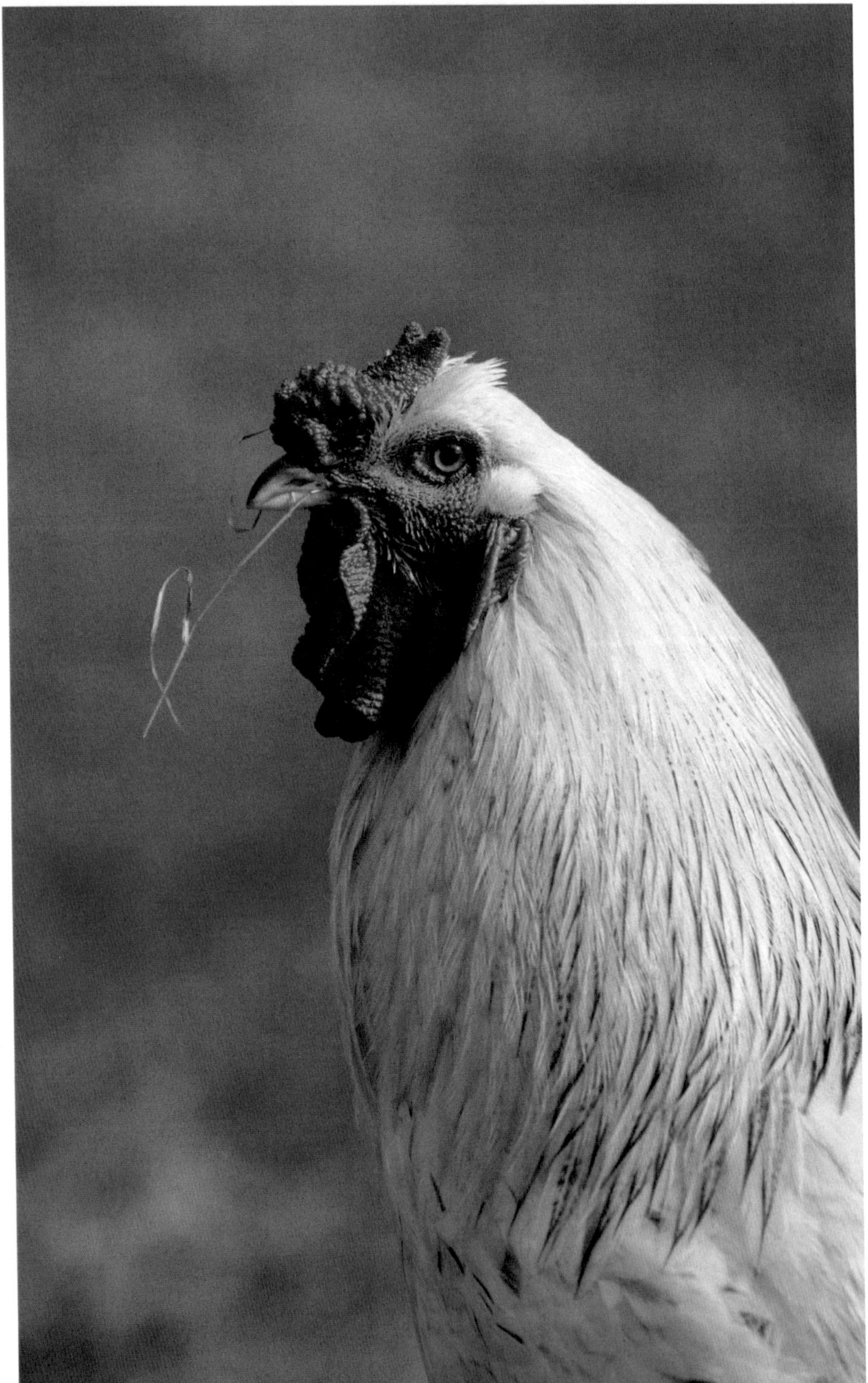

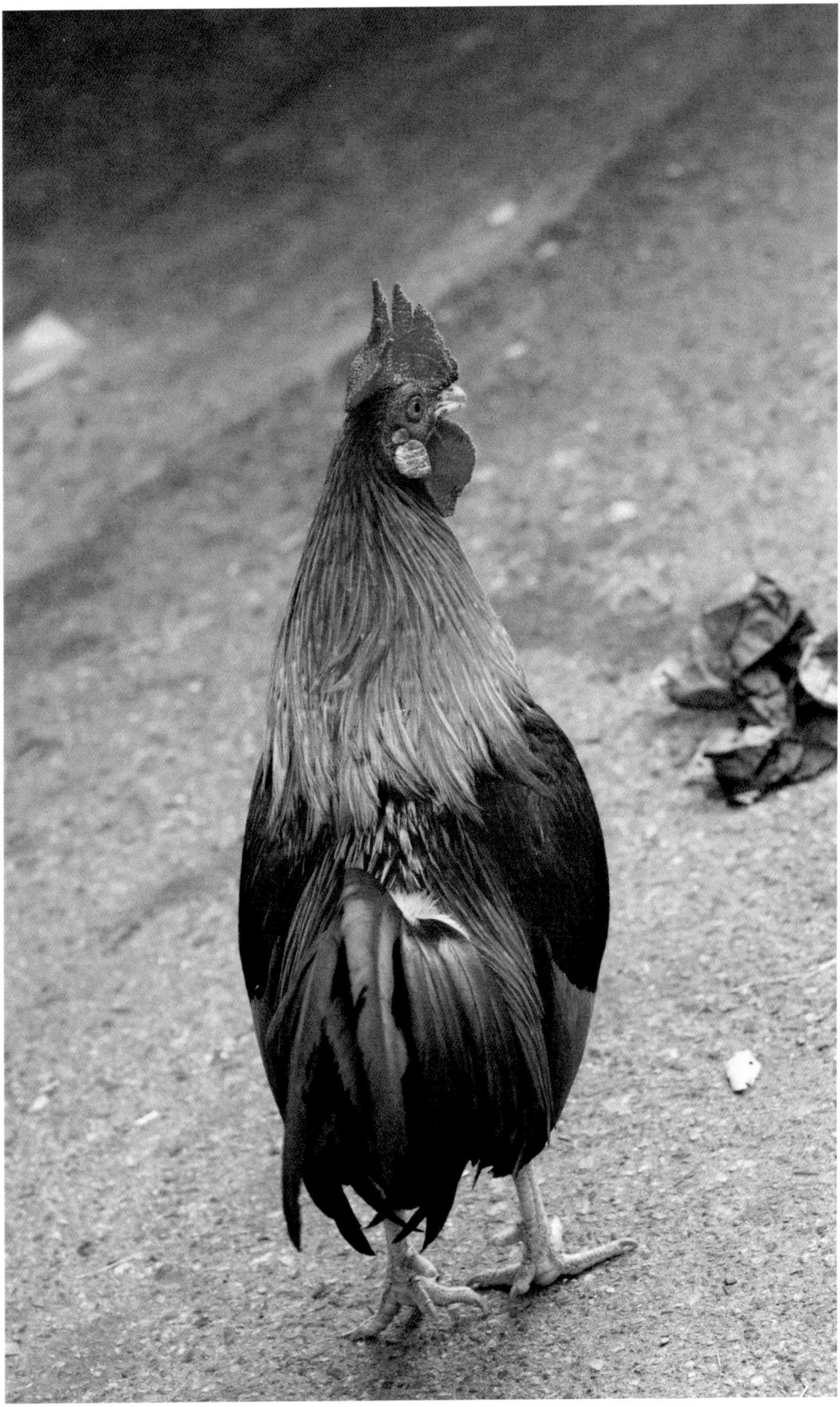

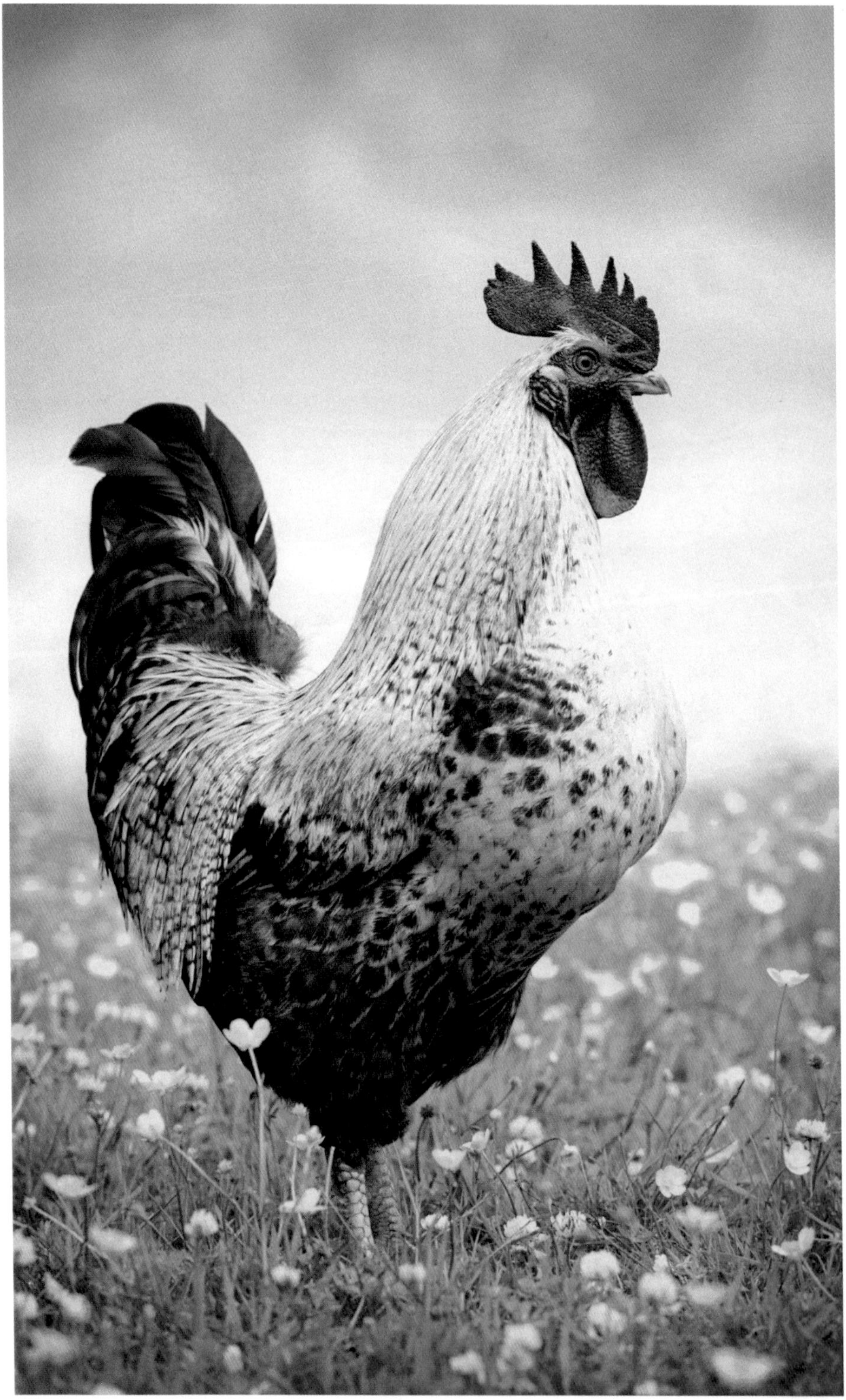

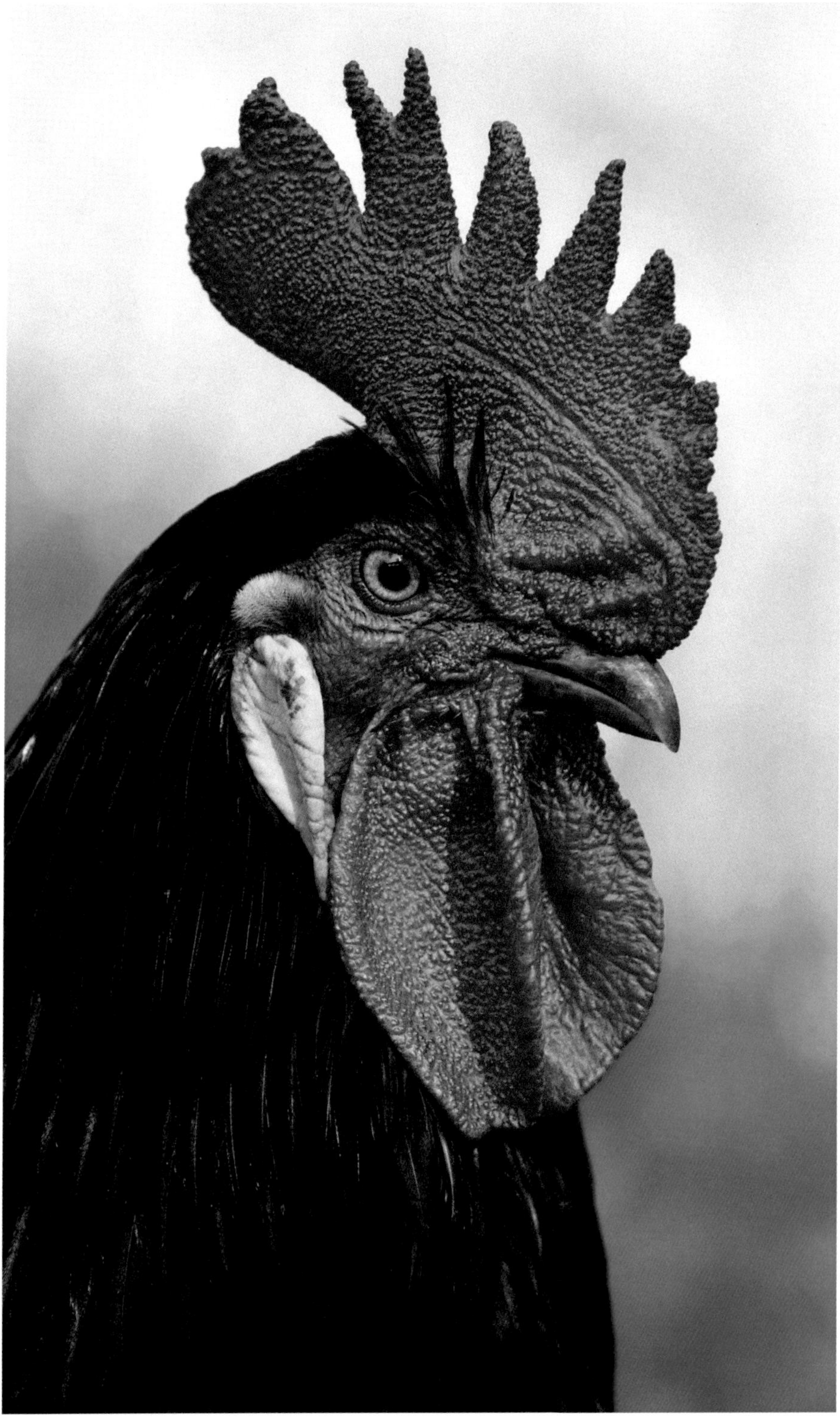

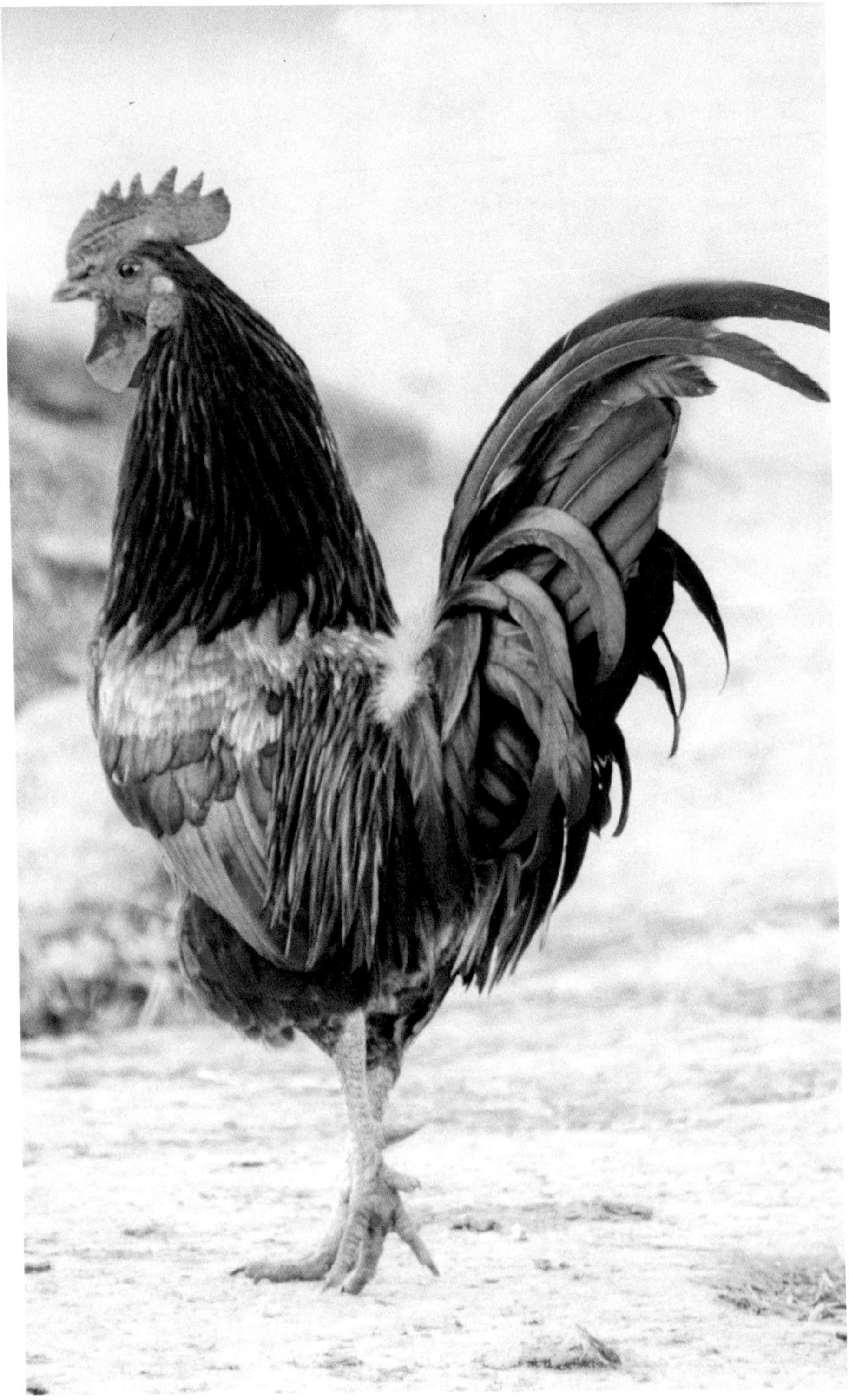

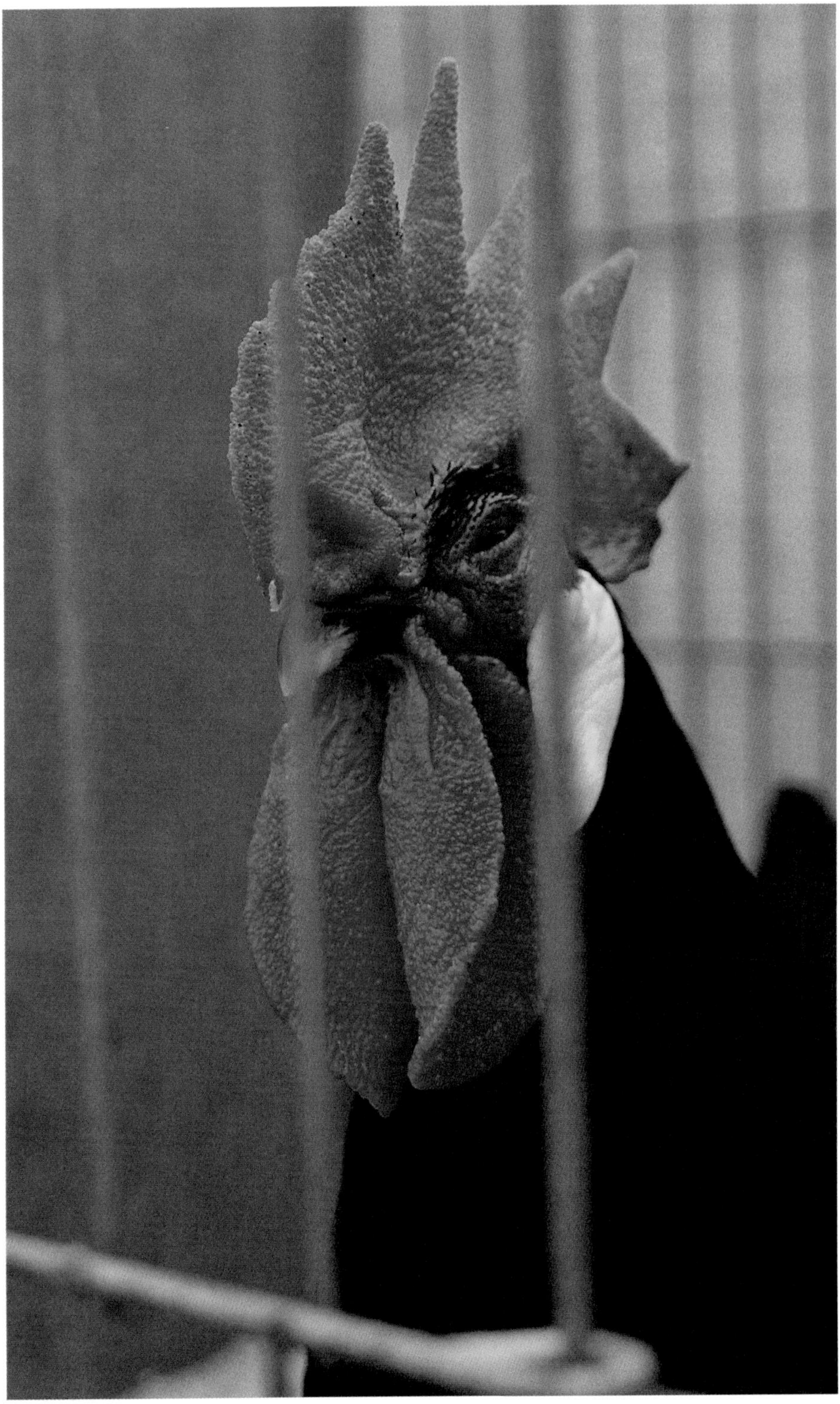

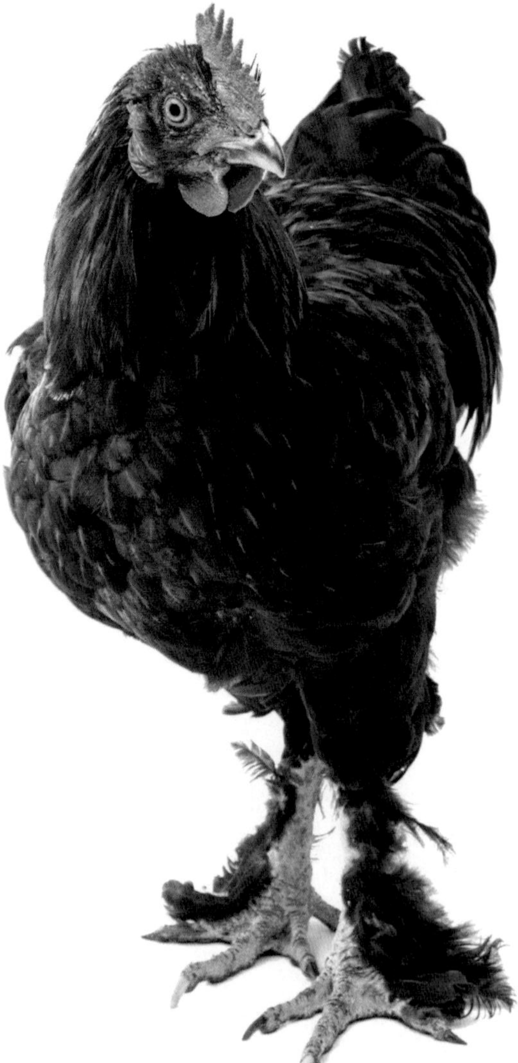

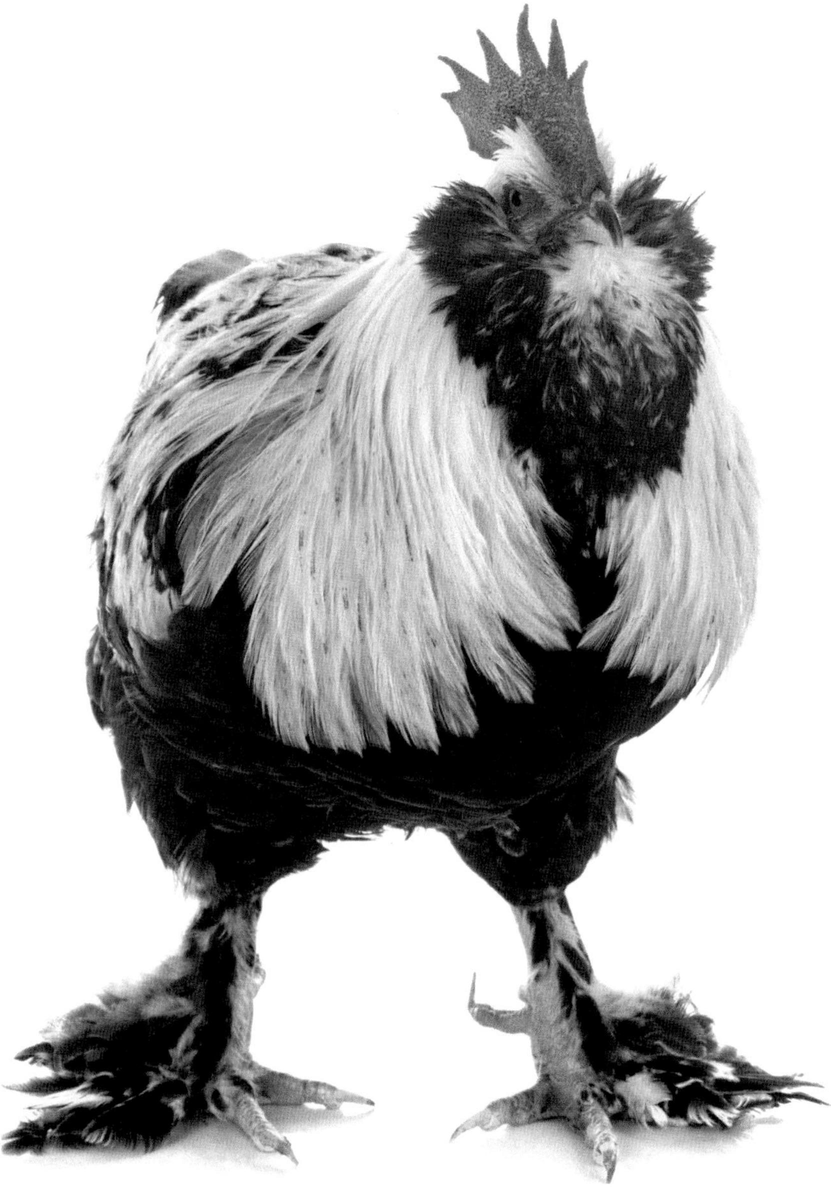

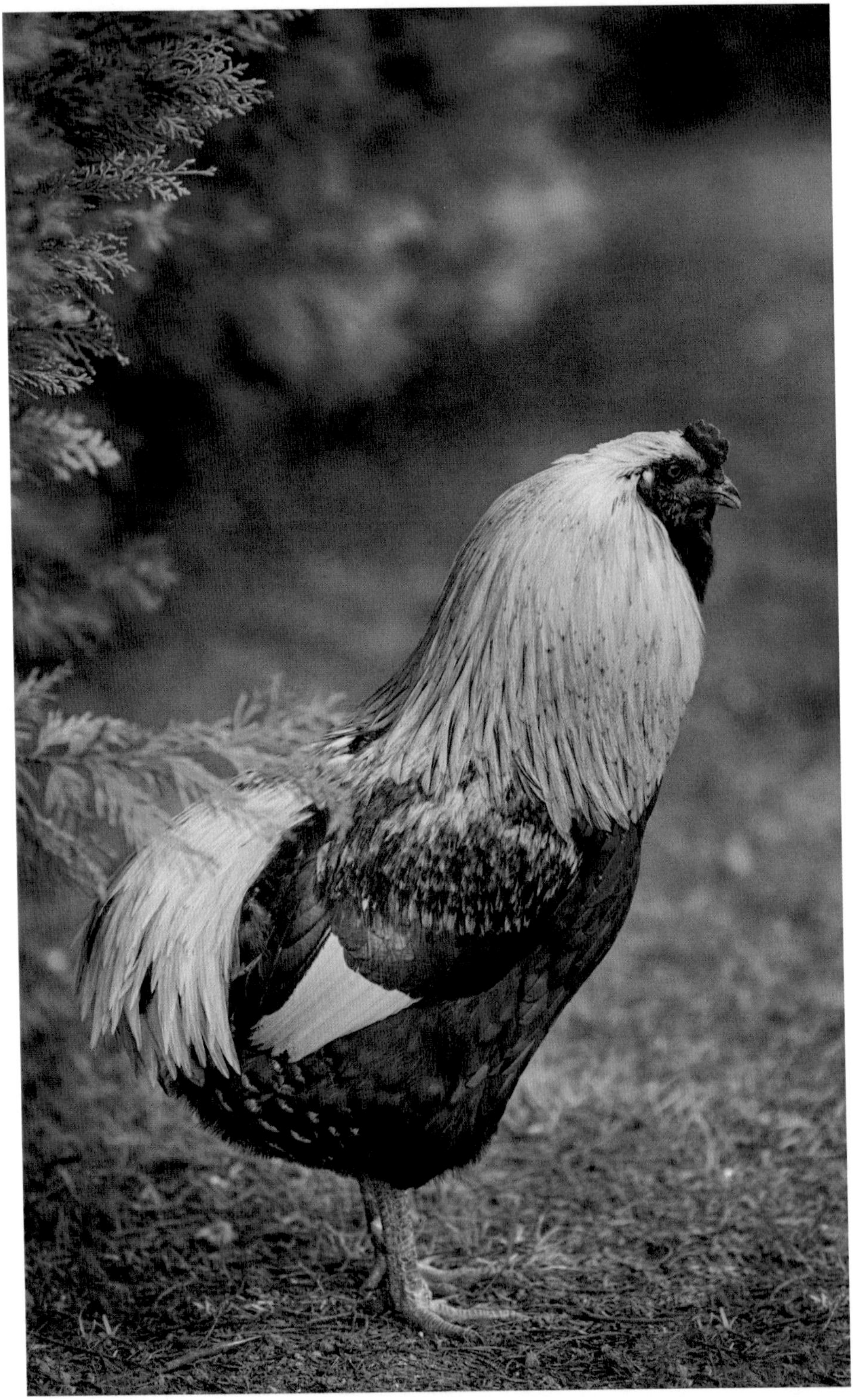

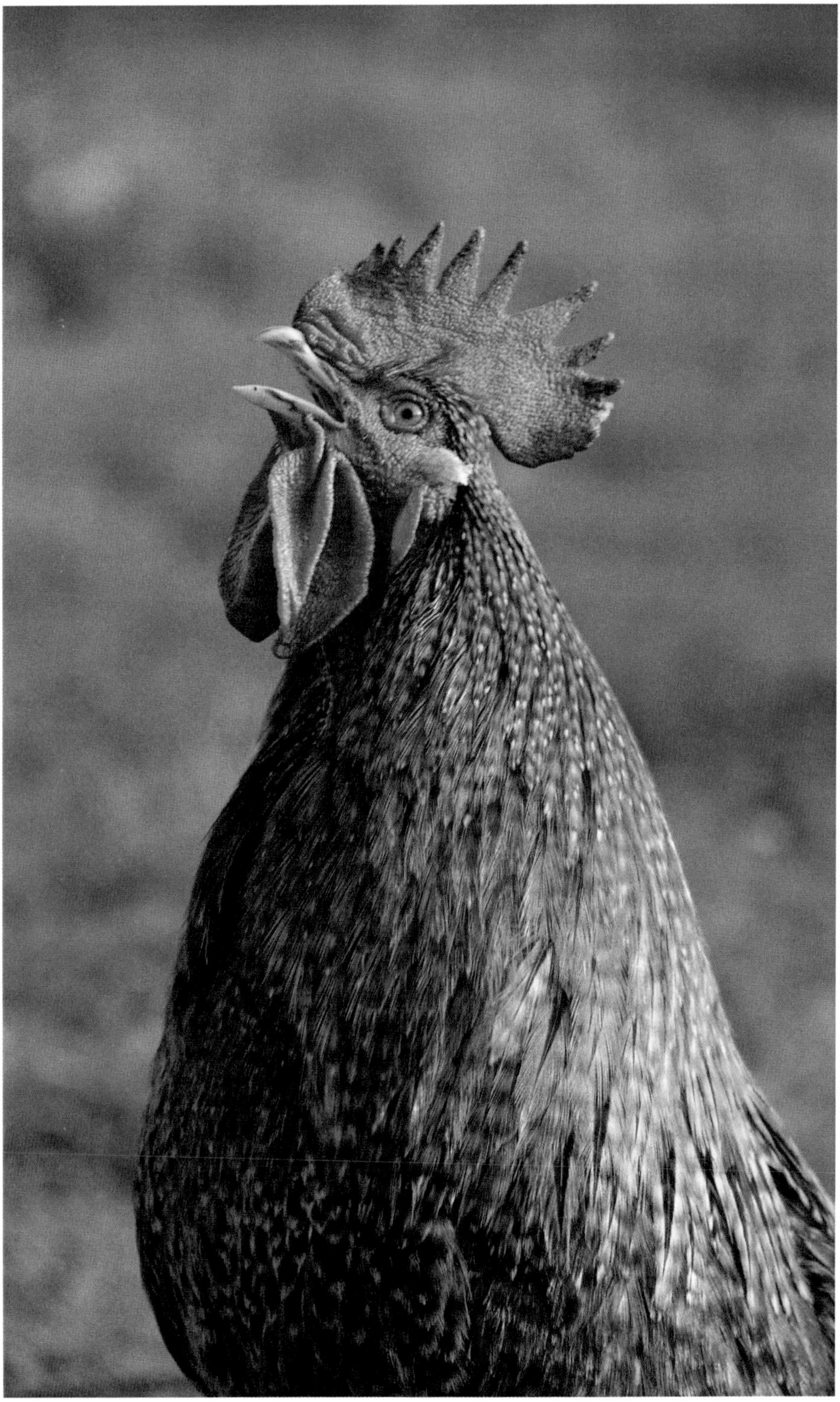

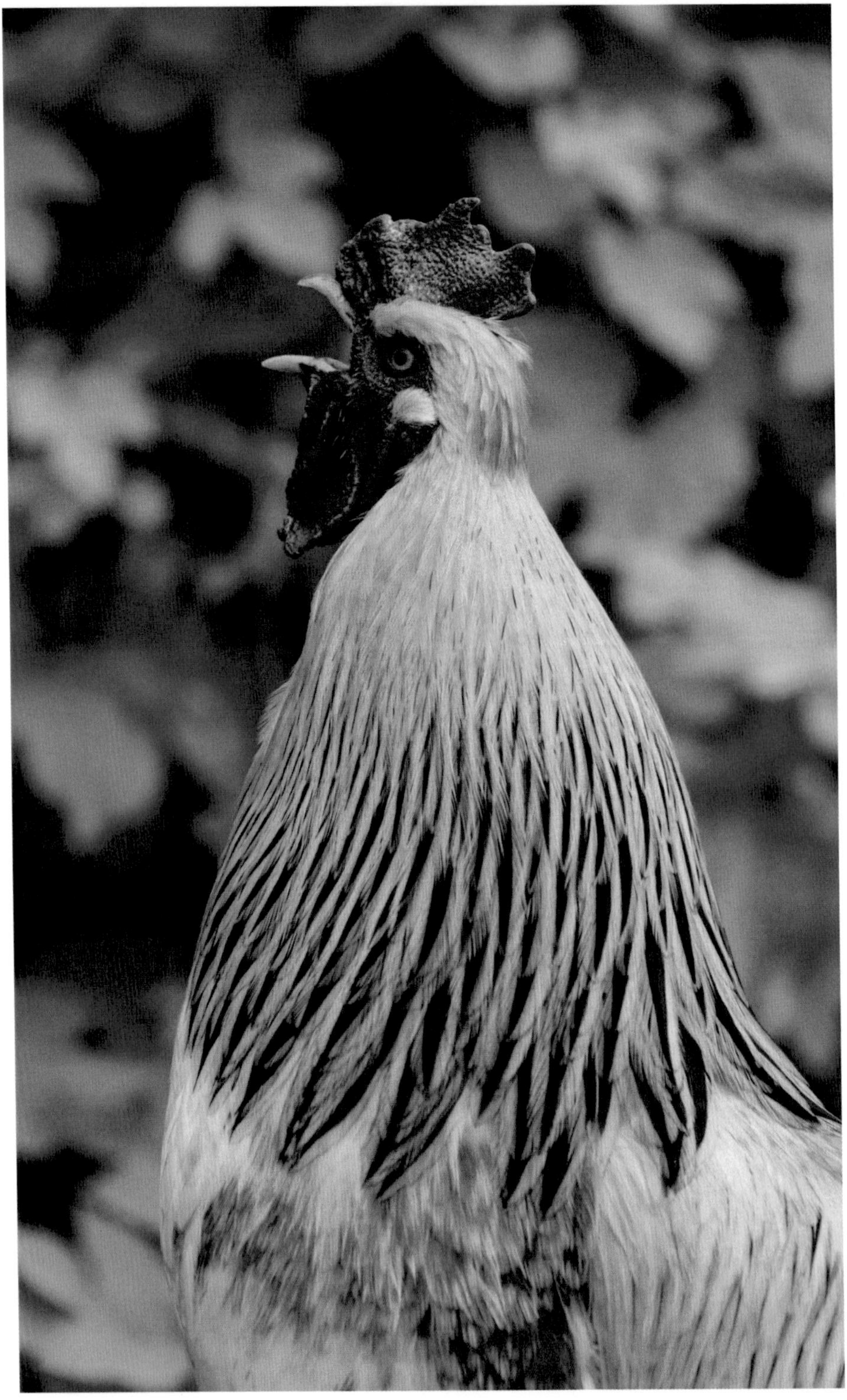

Made in the USA
Coppell, TX
09 December 2024

42077661R10026